WEREWOLVES

WEREWOLVES

Jon Izzard

Dedication

To all the charities and individuals throughout the world who are committed to the welfare of wolves and to their natural environment.

Caveat

While the text and illustrations may portray werewolves in a realistic way, the author asserts that the objective reality of werewolves should not be inferred from anything stated or depicted in this work. No part of this work should be regarded as offering recommendations that should be acted upon. Information on medical conditions, both physical and mental, is provided for entertainment only: seek professional medical advice if you have any concerns.

An Hachette UK Company
First published in Great Britain in 2009 by Spruce
a division of Octopus Publishing Group Ltd
2–4 Heron Quays, London E14 4JP
www.octopusbooks.co.uk
www.octopusbooksusa.com

Distributed in the U.S. and Canada
for Octopus Books USA
Hachette Book Group USA
237 Park Avenue
New York NY 10017

Produced by **Bookworx**
Editor: Jo Godfrey Wood, Designer: Peggy Sadler
Editorial assistant: Hannah Eiseman-Renyard

ISBN 13 978-1-84601-346-1
ISBN 10 1-84601-346-1

A CIP catalog record for this book is available from the British Library.

Printed and bound in China

10 9 8 7 6 5 4 3 2 1

CONTENTS

Introduction

If the werewolf signifies the beast within man—the beast that is eternally at odds with civilization—we are all werewolves. Whenever we are not enjoying absolute inner calm, we are experiencing the turbulence of the wolf prowling and growling within us. When we are annoyed and snap at somebody it is the wolf breaking surface and seizing control for an instant. When we lose our temper completely, the wolf is freed and pandemonium and destruction is unleashed.

The word "werewolf" is made up of a combination of two Old English words: *wer* meaning "man" and *wulf* meaning "wolf." Sometimes the combination of wolf and man is said to be physical, involving a dramatic and painful metamorphosis of the body from one form to the other.

Some people think that the transformation is metaphorical and insist the werewolf is a creature of myth, a fanciful or poetic description of how anger can erupt and take over our behavior. But others see the werewolf as a spiritual mystery; a supernatural creature composed of pure energy that can break free from our unguarded minds and wreak havoc in the lives of those we hate—or love.

We may pity the werewolf for his helplessness in the face of destiny; we may envy him his supernatural powers; we may fear him for his ferocity and lethal nature; or we may respect him for his long-suffering stoicism—but we can never ignore him. What is certain is that anyone unfortunate enough to encounter a werewolf will never sleep quite so easily again—especially on those nights when the wind howls and the full Moon looms strangely large, rising over the horizon of life's infinite possibilities...

THE BEAST UNLEASHED

Animal magnetism runs riot as Leon (Oliver Reed) reveals his darker side in *The Curse of the Werewolf* (1961). Under the spell of the full Moon, the werewolf transformation overpowers the doomed hero, who loses all self-control and becomes a brutal killer.

Chapter 1

Werewolves: The Beast Within

Men & Wolves

Our world makes us who we are, but deep within us lives the animal, dreaming of a world of scent and blood. Our ancestors were simple animals, but as the centuries went by we stood upright, invented tools, and became aware of ourselves.

HELPLESS HUMANS

Unlike most other animals, we are helpless when we are born because our bodies need more time to develop. However, a baby's head is already so large that to stay in the womb longer would make it very difficult for the mother to give birth. Our head, or brain, takes priority over our body.

Animal origins

Our brain's cerebral cortex has swollen with the powers of thought, reasoning, memory, and imagination, and it has expert control over the rest of our body. These things may not be so well developed in creatures such as the wolf, but the human brain still contains a primitive, animal core—the hypothalamus. This small part of the brain is about the size of an almond, but it controls our anger and our fatigue, our hunger and our thirst. Just like the wolf, our fight-or-flight response is triggered by this ancient part of the brain, which is common to all vertebrates.

We share many traits with the wolf. We both have predatory instincts, our societies are both hierarchical, and we are happiest and healthiest when we live in a pack (if only of two). We are both highly adapted to survive, yet in many ways the wolf is much tougher than we are: in a fight with an unarmed person, the wolf will almost certainly win. Men and wolves were rivals in the lean times when prey was scarce. Even after the great gray hunters became domesticated dogs, hunting with man rather than against him, that rivalry could all too easily come to the surface. Torn between cooperating and competing, we cover our wild side with a mask of "civilization" and coexist with our fellow creatures.

Different werewolves

It may be that there are several different sorts of werewolves in the world today. There is the physical werewolf, where the human body literally changes; the exotic spirit of the werewolf that exists independently of the body; and there is the fascinating werewolf of the mind, which we may come across as our "inner wolf."

ODIN, THE SCANDINAVIAN FATHER GOD

Odin's magical powers include shape-shifting, and as well as having two wolves, which are named Greedy and Ravenous, he has two ravens called Thought and Memory.

Werewolfism

The word "lycanthrope" (the Latinized form of the Greek *lukanthropos)* carries the same literal meaning as "werewolf," combining the words *lukos,* meaning wolf, and *anthropos,* meaning "man" (mankind).

Although lycanthropy is often used instead of the word "werewolfism," meaning the physical transformation of a man or woman into a wolf, lycanthropy is also a medical term used by psychologists for a complex set of symptoms caused by a psychosis, or madness.

Lycanthropy has a broad range of symptoms, varying from mild to serious. One woman, who was helped a great deal by medication, had a number of distressing symptoms although she hurt no one. Her story was published by doctors Rostenstock and Vincent in *The American Journal of Psychiatry*, October 1977.

The 49-year-old woman constantly felt inferior and needed a great deal of reassurance and affection. She was extremely interested in wolves, and these frequently cropped up in her dreams. Though her list of symptoms and characteristics do not show that anything was abnormal, her problem was how large they loomed in her life. She had overpoweringly low self-esteem, was obsessive, and completely fixated about wolves.

She had coped with this inner turmoil for decades, but her stability eventually broke down and, during a family get-together, she started to actually act out her dreadful compulsions.

Feeling herself overcome by the spirit of her "inner wolf," she stripped off all her clothes and started acting just like one. She hadn't been drinking alcohol or taking any drugs, but her mind's barriers had simply snapped under severe strain, allowing her repressed feelings to spill over into everyday life.

The following night, her wolf nature came to the fore again. This time the attack took place in her bedroom, where, growling, she scratched and chewed at the bed. Again it is the severity of the incident that is worth noting—it lasted for two whole hours.

Now seemingly beyond self-control, the woman was admitted to hospital. She complained about hearing voices and said that the Devil had entered her body. The doctors diagnosed her with lycanthropy. She said she was a wolf-woman by day and a wolf by night; that she was an animal with claws, hair, fangs, and snarling teeth. She also announced that she would continue to roam the Earth long after her death, continually searching for perfection and her own salvation.

Looking in a mirror, she often saw the head of a wolf instead of her own reflection, and that she would snarl and growl at herself, later saying the wolf had told her that it was the Devil. At other times, she would see her own face in the mirror, except that one eye looked frightened, while the other appeared to be that of a vicious wolf, deeply evil and filled with hatred of the other eye.

She was diagnosed with a chronic schizophrenic psychosis, so as well as receiving one-to-one psychotherapy she was given medication, which tackled the chemical imbalance in her brain that is the cause of schizophrenia. These frightening episodes stopped happening within a month, and when she looked in a mirror the wolf was gone.

The woman's symptoms calmed down and, after she had received treatment for nine weeks, she was released from hospital. The doctors were convinced that she had been on the verge of suicide, but that she was now firmly on the road to recovery.

Lycanthropy is not restricted to schizophrenia, but may appear as a symptom of depression, bipolar disorder, drug-induced toxic psychosis, hysterical neurosis, psychomotor epilepsy, or physical changes in the brain due to, for example, a tumor. As such, lycanthropy is not a diagnosis in itself, but identifying it helps to make a more complete diagnosis.

An insightful novel that explores the theme of the inner struggle between man and wolf, civilization and chaos, matter and spirit, is *Steppenwolf* (*Der Steppenwolf,* 1927) by Hermann Hesse, who went on to win the Nobel Prize for Literature.

The story follows Harry Haller, a man who regards himself as part wolf—a lost, lone wolf of the steppes. Nursing his split personality, Harry daily confronts the double standards and hypocrisy at the heart of his world. His continual efforts to balance the polar opposites in his life reveal his own humanity and make him a hero in a unique mold, like all true heroes.

The media often uses phrases relating to werewolves when describing particularly vicious attacks involving mutilation or cannibalism, even when there is no evidence of lycanthropy. For example, William Johnston was dubbed the "Werewolf of San Francisco" in the 1930s because he cut his victims with a bladed weapon and the wounds were said to resemble claw marks. And the notorious "Wolf Man" of London, Michael Lupo, simply derived his nickname from his surname, which meant wolf. He was convicted of killing four people in 1986 and died in prison.

The Body of the Werewolf

PHYSICAL CHANGES

Most of the werewolves in movies, books, and games physically change from ordinary men and women into wolves. Our everyday experience shows us that caterpillars transform into butterflies, and genetically modified foods combine different species into new hybrid organisms. So who's to say physical werewolves are pure fiction?

Origins

The earliest stories of werewolves, such as Homer's tale of Circe (see page 128), the enchantress turning men into wolves, and the tale of King Lycaon in Arcadia (see facing page) who was turned into a wolf by an angry god, involve physical transformation. But even those early Greek sources are not in complete agreement on the nature of the beast.

The earliest of these stories, written around 2,800 years ago, tell that the men bewitched by Circe had the bodies of wolves, but they kept the minds of men. When Odysseus's seafarers arrived, the wolves did not hungrily attack them like a pack of wild animals, but greeted them as companions in the spirit of human friendship.

Another example that shows werewolves in their wolf form behaving like people comes from medieval Ireland, where the werewolves of Ossory (see pages 102–3) actually talk to people (these are unusual, though, because under their wolf's skin they still remain human physically). Other examples are the werewolves in the stories of *Bisclavret* (see page 143) and *William and the Werewolf* (see page 146). Both these tales are medieval romances. And even the 1985 movie *Teen Wolf* (see pages 90–3), with its fun-loving werewolf, is a romantic comedy.

Losing control

The wolf with a human heart, however, is a rare breed. The vast majority of werewolves in literature, both ancient and modern, stress the complete loss of humanity that accompanies the physical change: this is the bestial wolf, the true predator. A classic example is the 1941 movie *The Wolf Man* (see pages 69–72), where the werewolf in his human form knows he must leave the woman he loves rather than risk killing her in his wolf form. The earlier movie (from

LYCAON INTO WOLF

King Lycaon killed and cooked a prisoner, and fed the meat to his guest. But the guest was the god Zeus in disguise, and he punished Lycaon by turning him into a wolf.

1935) *Werewolf of London* (see pages 78–80) suggests a glimmer of self-control at the moment the werewolf is about to attack his beloved wife, but even that possibility is left deliberately vague.

CHANGING BACK

Another feature common to both the completely bestial wolf and the wolf with a human heart, is that there is the ability to change back into human form. The monthly change at the full Moon is the most obvious example, where the wolf form lasts for just a few hours overnight. But even the older stories, such as that told of the Anthus clan (see page 137), where men became wolves for nine years at a time, or the werewolves of Ossory, who became wolves for seven years, offer the definite possibility to become human once more.

Open curse

Sometimes the curse of being in their wolf form is open-ended, and the extreme case of Lycaon, who was doomed to live as a wolf for the rest of his life, could have ended differently, as the evil king could have been pardoned and restored to human form if Zeus had simply changed his mind. The so-called first generation of Lycans in the *Underworld* series of movies (see pages 57–9), is unusual because there is no possibility of becoming human.

DRESSED TO KILL 

Rock star Ozzy Osbourne undergoes a theatrical transformation in this photo shoot for his solo album *Bark at the Moon* (1983). The title track is about a werewolf who rises from his grave, seeking revenge.

PERIODIC CHANGE

Return from the wolf phase to the human race was permanent in the cases of the Anthus clan and Sir Marrok of Arthurian legend (see page 144), but mostly it was periodic. Usually, the change from human to wolf and back again, was forced by circumstance. Often this event is as inevitable as the waxing of the Moon. At other times the change can be voluntary.

Choice and control

As we'll see, there may be ways of controlling the transformation, either by conscious choice or by magic such as the Devil's belt or girdle, supposedly used in the case of Peter Stubbe the 16th-century German farmer, otherwise known as the "Werewolf of Bedburg" (see pages 156–60). In his trial it was stated that putting the belt on would instantly make him a wolf, while removing it would return him to his human body.

Change for show

Performers, such as actors and some singers, routinely change their personality and become—or seem to become—somebody else on stage. Imagining ourselves to be a different person is a natural part of imaginative play in childhood. But sometimes even professional actors find it difficult to step out of character and leave their imaginary lives behind, to return to normal life.

The Spirit of the Werewolf

THE NATURE OF SPIRIT

Many people have only a hazy idea of what "spirit" is. It just seems vague and "religious," and doesn't seem to have any impact on daily life. We may be forgiven for our ignorance. After all, the questions of what spirit is and how it works have challenged philosophers and mystics for millennia. Meanwhile, there are plenty of people who don't think that spirit exists at all.

The potent human spirit

Many kinds of spirit have been described—some holy and others evil; some that exist in the world at large and others that exist in every human being. Ideas about the spirit of the werewolf fall into just a few types. When occultists talk about the "spirit of the werewolf," they usually describe it as part of the human being that, uniquely, can move outside the physical body and operate independently of it. It is clearly a powerful and potentially dangerous thing.

THE BODIES

This spirit is most often described as the "astral body," but other terms used in connection with the werewolf include the "sidereal body," "the etheric body," "the subtle body," "the body of desire," "the body of passion," "the dream body," "the odic body," "the body of light," and even simply "ghost." Students of the occult arts recognize all the technical distinctions between the various terms, and several may exist all at once in the same person. The different names usually describe how evolved the various spiritual bodies are. For example, the sidereal body is more refined than the body of passion. But there is general agreement that these terms all describe something real and are not just metaphorical. And, crucially, everybody has at least one.

The astral body

For convenience we'll use the generic term "astral body" unless we are specifically referring to one of the other sorts. The astral body is said to be composed of an immaterial or "unphysical" substance that is normally contained within the physical body, but which may leave it sometimes, either voluntarily or involuntarily. This astral body is capable of moving around the world freely and, sometimes, interacting with it physically.

Other animal forms

The werewolf in *Camp of the Dog* (see pages 148–50) is exactly this sort of creature. The shape or appearance of the astral body is determined by the forces that dominate it; in this case, a wolf. In countries where the main predator is not a wolf but, say, the jaguar or the tiger, those animals would be the natural way a person chooses to express their more aggressive, predatory spirit, and that animal would form the shape of the astral body. There is a strong link between this body and the physical body. If this link is cut, the results could be very serious. Wounds sustained

The Sentinel

The 1996 TV series, *The Sentinel,* is a fascinating glimpse into how a human being with an animal's enhanced abilities can adjust to living in the modern world.

James Ellison, a captain in the US Special Forces, develops immensely heightened senses while he is in the Peruvian jungle. Five years later, and a plain-clothes detective with the Major Crimes Unit in Cascade, Washington, he suddenly finds his senses awakening and, unable to cope with the sensory input, seeks medical help. He meets Blair Sandford, an anthropology student masquerading as a doctor, who tells him he is a Sentinel—a human with enhanced senses who in ancient times took on the role of protector of his tribe and territory.

Blair knows how to help Jim control and manage his extraordinary abilities, and the two become unofficial partners. Jim's "spirit animal" is a black jaguar, while Blair's is a wolf: they are able, in an emergency, to communicate via their spirit animals.

on the astral plane by the astral body may also affect or show up on the physical body.

MANIFESTATION

Most spirit werewolves manifest without actually intending to, usually at night while the person is asleep. Some occultists practice exercises that are intended to bring about the release of the astral body, allowing them to explore the spiritual world, and the shape they choose is benign (they may either choose their own human form, or that of a glowing sphere, for example).

Psychic umbilical cord

In her textbook *Psychic Self Defense* (1930) Dion Fortune describes what happened to her one afternoon while she was thinking vengeful thoughts about what to do about somebody who had done her wrong. She felt a tugging at her solar plexus and from this point came a psychic umbilical cord that was attached to the body of a large wolf materializing beside her.

Ectoplasm

The wolf was formed out of ectoplasm flowing from her body, and she struggled to reabsorb it quickly to prevent the wolf dashing off to perform its mission of savage revenge. As the last of the ectoplasm was reintegrated within herself, she was filled with an almost overwhelming rage in which she could have easily ripped apart anyone within reach.

RITUALS

The conjuring of a non-corporeal, or non-physical wolf can, according to occult lore, also be achieved through ceremony and ritual. These thought-forms do not come directly out of the magician that conjures them, but are built up from the spiritual energy or "astral light" that fills the Universe.

The magician

Rather as a potter might mold a vessel on the potter's wheel, the magician forms an appropriate body (in this case a wolf's), but instead of clay, the shape is composed of the spiritual energy that is the astral plane. Once it is formed into the appropriate shape and size, this astral wolf is filled with the desires of the magician, who directs it toward its target.

Once created, the thought-form of the wolf is released, and is expected to act independently to carry out its mission. If the magician is intent on vengeance, the werewolf might, for example, stalk the victim's dreams, turning them to nightmares. Or it might be responsible for a

NATIVE AMERICAN ARAPAHO WOLF MASK

When wolves were reintroduced to Yellowstone Park, Wyoming, USA, in 1995, the Northern Arapaho Wolf Society celebrated with their sacred Wolf Dance. This man at the Buffalo Bill Historical Center, Wyoming, wears a wolf headdress.

plague of irritating accidents that eat away at the victim's health and enjoyment of life. The attack may even, so it is said, end up in a brutal death. Such werewolves clearly fall in the province of black magic and operate along similar lines to a voodoo curse, instilling terror deep in the victim's subconscious mind.

Damaging rituals

But there are tales in which rituals conjure demonic wolves that do very real damage. In his 1595 book *Demonolatry,* which largely replaced the *Malleus Maleficarum* as the handbook of choice for the European witch-finders in the 16th century, the French magistrate Nicolas Remy told the story of Petrone Armentarius and Joannes Malrisius. Inspired by jealousy of a neighbor's flocks, the men would tear up some grass, throw it against the trunk of a tree, and say a spell. Immediately a demonic wolf would spring forth and carry out a vicious attack on the designated sheep. This, they confessed, they did often.

Benign effects

Of course, magicians may have good rather than evil intentions. For example, they might want to create a fierce protector and to conjure up a wolf to nurture the wellbeing of themselves or any person who would benefit from an invisible yet powerful ally. Such a furred guardian would be intended to be a positive benefit, and its purpose would, in the view of most occultists, commend it as "white" magic. Magicians tend to agree that what distinguishes white from black magic, and good from evil magic, is the purpose for which the spell is cast.

DANGER ON THE ASTRAL PLANE

But in occult lore, humans are not the only beings capable of manipulating the astral planes. Neo-Theosophist C.W. Leadbetter describes another danger that may harm an apprentice occultist, especially when learning the technique of astral projection. In his book *The Astral Plane: Its Scenery, Inhabitants and Phenomena* (1895), he warns that the occultist's astral body may be attacked by other astral entities and forced to take on the form of a wolf. In this degraded form it may rove, thirsty for blood, and keen to kill—following the nature of the entities that have possessed the unprotected occultist's astral body.

This comes close to echoing some of the theories of medieval theologians, who in place of the neutral word "entity" would substitute the word "devil." For example, the influential cleric Pierre Mamor wrote in his *Flagellum Maleficorum* (published around 1490, but written some 30 years earlier) that the werewolf that attacks livestock and murders men, women, and children, is actually an ordinary, physical wolf that has been possessed by the Devil.

MEN INTO BEASTS

The infamous witch-hunting guide *Malleus Maleficarum* (1487) of Heinrich Kramer and James Sprenger tackled the question of whether witches can change men into beasts. It refers to werewolves, and includes the story of a man who often left his home to hide in some local caves. There he slept and dreamed that he was ravaging the countryside, devouring children. Despite believing that he was responsible, it was actually the Devil that possessed a natural wolf and caused the destruction. Eventually, the man was driven to madness. In this way the Devil obtains two victims at once: the one physically attacked, and the person who is asleep somewhere near by who believes that they are responsible for the attack. Perhaps the sleeper will actually dream about the attack, with their imagination imprinted by the Devil's art; or maybe they will simply assume that they are responsible when they cannot produce a satisfactory alibi.

FOREST DEMON

This creature was said to inhabit forests around Salzburg, Austria, and Hamburg, Germany, and was thought to be a witch wearing an uncured skin in a primitive rite, which could have given rise to the werewolf legend. This woodcut was made in 1669.

Montague Summers
THE WEREWOLF
IN
LORE AND LEGEND

Mamor also recognizes another form of werewolf, and cites Saint Augustine as his authority. Again the human in the drama is asleep or entranced by a diabolical spell, but in this version the spirit of the dreamer actually possesses the body of the ordinary wolf, spurring it on to perform its savage work. In this case, any shepherd found sleeping on the job while a wolf attacks his flock is liable to find himself in very deep trouble indeed.

THE FAMILIAR GHOST

The sort of spirit most people have heard the most about is the ghost. Montague Summers, in his influential book *The Werewolf* (1933), offers two ghost stories with a werewolf theme.

When the infamous English King John died in 1216, he was buried inside Worcester Cathedral, but he failed to rest in peace. Howling, shrieks, and unholy commotions were heard around his grave, and continued until the canons of the cathedral disinterred him and cast his corpse into unconsecrated ground. After that, his ghost was seen in the form of a werewolf, arousing great fear among local people.

A BOOK WITH BITE

Front cover of the Dover edition of *The Werewolf in Lore and Legend* (2003), an unabridged reprint of the 1933 classic *Werewolf* by the Catholic priest Montague Summers, who believed in the literal transformation of werewolves.

This item of popular folklore seems to be unfounded, at least regarding the exhumation. According to *An Account of the Discovery of the Body of King John* (1797), by Valentine Green, his royal tomb was opened and his bones found to be intact. However, it is worth noting that King John's tomb in the cathedral was next to his favorite saint, Saint Wulfstan (1008–1095), or "Wolf-stone."

A punished king

The other ghost story is from the war-torn area of the Somme, northern France. In 1131 Hugues III of Campdavaine, the Count of Saint-pol, destroyed the abbey of Saint-Riquier, killing refugees and clergy alike by sword and fire.

Despite agreeing with Pope Innocent II six years later that he should build three new abbeys in reparation, his soul was apparently far from free from the guilt. Following his death in 1141, Hugues's ghost was seen in the form of a black wolf, heavily laden with metal chains, roaming around the abbey of Saint-Riquier, and howling in the night.

Crimes against the Church

Both Hugues and King John were judged to have committed truly awful crimes against the Church (King John was excommunicated by Pope Innocent III between 1209 and 1213). That people who reported seeing their ghosts described them as werewolves (rather than Earth-bound souls in ordinary, God-given human form), clearly reveals what kind of men they were both perceived to be. Ravening wolves indeed.

Learning From the Wolf

THE COLLECTIVE CONSCIOUSNESS
Right down the centuries, both wolves and werewolves have had an enormous influence on the collective consciousness of mankind.

Naming after wolves
One of the most obvious manifestations of this is the number of first names that are derived from "wolf" (see box below). In addition, there are many phrases connected with wolves that have passed into the language (see box page 30).

A thousand years ago, the wolf's reputation as a fear-inspiring and powerful adversary had such an influence that parents often named their children after wolves. However, there is a distinct sexual asymmetry, with the great majority of wolf names being given to boys.

Two-fold message
Presumably, such names had a two-fold message: a warning to all to treat the bearer with respect, and to give the child a role model to live up to.

Wolf Names

Wolves have inspired many first names. Here are some examples:

- *Wolf Power (Germanic)—Ulric (male); Ulrica (female).*
- *Wolf Strong (Irish)—Conall (male).*
- *Noble Wolf (Germanic)—Adolf, Adolphus, Aethelwulf, Dolph (male); Adolphina, Adolpha (female).*
- *Wolf Lord (Irish)—Whiltierna (female).*
- *Fame Wolf (Germanic)—Rudolf, Rolf, Rudy (male).*
- *Rim (of a Shield) Wolf (Germanic)—Randolf, Randal, Randolph, Randy (male); Randi (female).*
- *Counsel Wolf (Germanic)—Ralph, Rafe, Raoul (male); Ralphina, Ralphine (female).*
- *Advice Wolf (Scandinavian)—Ranulf (male).*
- *Wolf Going (Germanic)—Wolfgang (male).*
- *Wolf Valley (Spanish)—Guadalupe, Lupita, Lupe, Lupelina (female).*
- *Wolf (Norse)—Lyall (male).*
- *Wolf (Irish)—Phelan (male).*
- *Wolf (Germanic)—Woolf, Wolfe (male).*
- *Small Wolf (Welsh)—Bleddyn (male).*
- *Wolf-cub (French)—Lovell, Lovel (male).*

These parental yearnings spawned a great many striking names.

Totem deity

There is a third possibility, also, that the parents were placing their child under the protection of a totem deity. The novel *Wolf Totem* by Jiang Rong dramatizes the relationship the nomadic people of Inner Mongolia, China, have with "the sons of

A WOLF AT THE DOOR

Like many Christians, artists often use the wolf to represent evil. In this political cartoon, the wolf is the terror of starvation that visited so many families in Ireland under English rule. The poor here are rescued by Erin, the heroic spirit of Ireland.

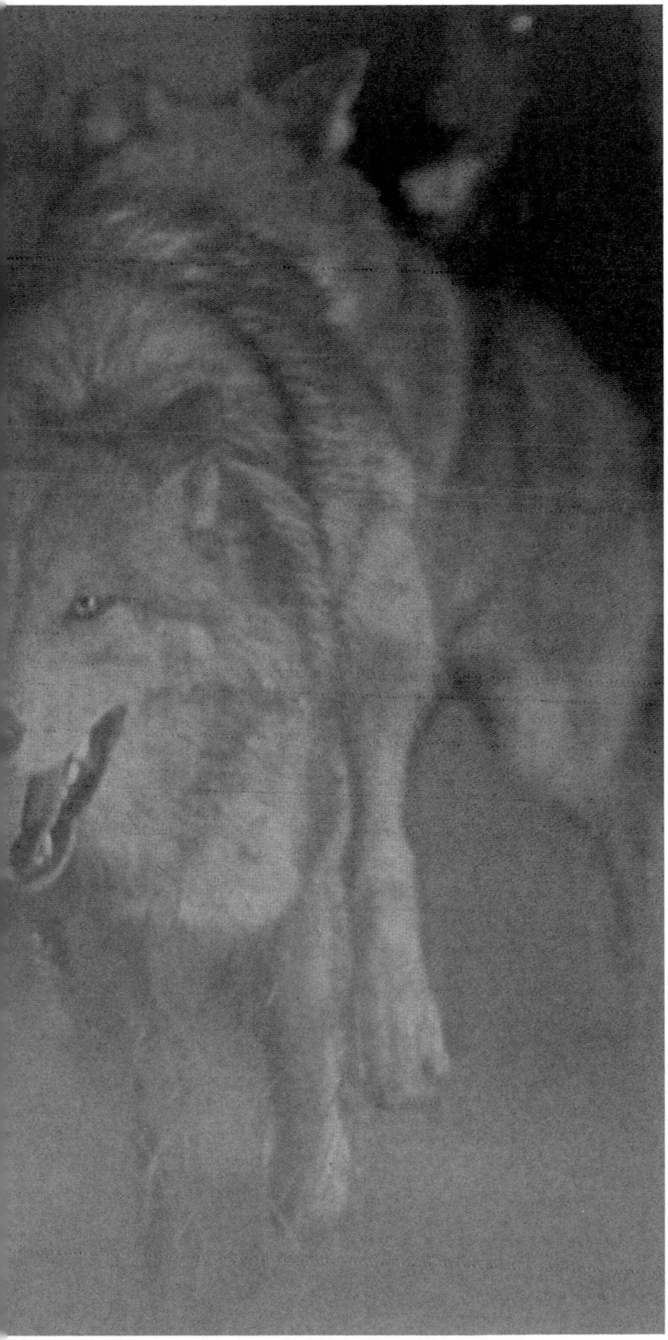

the sky" wolves. They do not fear the power of the wolf but embrace it—they regard the wolf as embodying all the elements needed to survive in the steppe. For them the wolf is a positive influence, both spiritually and on a practical level, as it helps maintain a balanced ecosystem there. The book contrasts the harsh yet noble lives of the nomads, with the peaceful and settled existences of people in agricultural communities, comparing the farmers to sheep who fear both the people of the steppe and their totem, the wolf.

Wolf in human clothing

It is a sad irony that many people in the business community bought into the book's ethos of the wolf totem, seeing themselves mirrored in the image of the untamed predator. After all, the book was intended to help protect the environment threatened by exploitation, not make the situation worse by encouraging that exploitation.

The success of *Wolf Totem* was followed by several self-help books specifically aimed at businessmen, teaching them how to get ahead in business by becoming wolves in suits.

GRAY WOLVES 

Canis lupus, the gray wolf, ranges across much of Eurasia and North America; and so does the traditional werewolf, although, with the advent of modern transport, it is possible that werewolves may be found almost anywhere.

Wolfish Expressions

Most personality traits that are described in terms of the wolf tend to be a little insulting and are usually related to preying on someone or something. Common expressions include:

- *The "wolf at the door" is the bringer of ruin, starvation, and death.*
- *To "throw someone to the wolves" is to condemn or abandon them to utter ruin.*
- *To "wolf down" food is to eat fast and greedily.*
- *A "wolf's lair" is the base or headquarters of a sinister or scheming person.*
- *A "wolf" may be a violent or rapacious person, or simply a womanizer.*
- *The offensive "wolf whistle" declares that animal passions have been aroused.*
- *A "wolf pack" may mean any gang of predators and was used to translate the German word* rudeltaktik *(literally "pack tactic"), which described the Nazi policy of using a group of submarines (U-boats) to hunt allied shipping convoys in World War II.*
- *To "cry wolf" is to raise a false alarm deliberately.*
- *A "wolf in sheep's clothing" is a predatory deception.*
- *A "wolf note" is an imperfect contribution or contributor.*

A true guide

At a more holistic level, the wolf totem inspires us with its tough determination, never-ending patience, prompt adaptability, disciplined teamwork, and its capacity for supreme self sacrifice for the sake of the pack. The wolf is a true guide and pathfinder; it is a great teacher, strong and wise.

LIVING IN THE NOW

Part of the wolf's overall appeal revolves around "living in the now." The world we presently live in moves faster than our minds and bodies can comfortably cope with—part of the reason why too many people feel stressed for far too much of the time.

"The now of wolf-thought," as Wendy and Richard Pini express it in their *ElfQuest* series of graphic novels (1978, ongoing), requires the mind to focus only on what is happening at this minute. There is no fretting over the past; no worrying about the future. "Now" is what really matters. It's the wonderful and timeless immediacy of childhood and can be useful if you are trying to reduce your stress levels.

The destructive rage of the werewolf

Living in the now is also particularly relevant to the overarching theme of the werewolf—the sudden, violent release of utter rage in the transformation that overcomes us when we lose our temper. The murderous, frenzied attacks associated with the worse cases of the medical condition lycanthropy offer a vivid reminder of what can happen when raw destruction comes to the surface and erupts.

Anger management

Paradoxically, the wolf can be useful in anger management, as the animal would not waste its time and energy raving against something that is either so big that it's out of our control, or so small that we simply shouldn't bother about it. Though ferocious, the wolf is a creature with a clear sense of proportion.

Standing up for ourselves

The wolf can help us become more assertive. In the highly structured world of school, work, and social life, we can become too passive, too willing to roll over and give up. Sometimes we need to stand up for what we believe in, even if we stand alone. The lone wolf is not afraid, neither is it out of control. It is intensely alive and self-aware.

The best outcome

Being assertive allows us to express opposition without actually being aggressive. Although it involves confrontation, it is not about winning, but rather about solving a problem and finding the best outcome.

Self assertion—finding a good balance between being a doormat and being overly aggressive—is a weapon that can be wielded with disarming gentleness. Using the power of our inner wolf can transform our lives in a very positive way.

Bisclavret

In the French romance *Bisclavret* (see page 143), the werewolf greets his old friend the king so graciously that the king immediately realizes he is no ordinary wolf. Then the king adopts him as a pet, and that's how things continue for a long time.

It is only when the werewolf attacks the two people who have treacherously condemned him to his werewolf life—in other words, when he actually starts behaving like a wolf—that the king discovers the truth. And, at last, the werewolf is able to revert to human shape.

The wolf's lesson

The most profound lesson of the wolf as a totem is one of transformation. Learning the best of everything the wolf has to teach us can produce self-transformation.

Liberating transformations

Then, with a clear vision of ourselves and our lives, we are in a much better position to transform our environment. These liberating transformations are only possible when they are tempered with a wholehearted commitment to taking personal responsibility for ourselves and our actions.

The Beast-Man Strikes

A "therianthrope" is, literally, a beast-man, a were-creature. The word is not only used to describe werewolves but all shape-shifters who transform between human and animal.

The werewolf is the tip of a very large iceberg. Tales of therianthropy may be found all around the world and make a fascinating study. Many have a clear resonance with werewolves. For instance, Kitsune (see below) would fit snugly into the werewolf category if her animal was a wolf instead of a fox.

ANIMAL GODS

Perhaps the best-known images that combine human and animal features are the Egyptian gods, for example Anubis, who is portrayed as being mostly human but possessing the head of a jackal. Most other animals are represented in the pantheon, and these range from crocodiles (Sobek) to falcons (Horus). And the famous giant sphinx at Giza is the body of a lion, but with a human head.

SHAPE-SHIFTING

In shamanic traditions, the experienced shaman is able to transform into a wide variety of forms, including wolves.

Nagual

In Meso-America, for example, the nocturnal shape-shifting abilities of the *nagual* (or *nahual*, often translated as "transforming witch") are typical in their diversity, with animals ranging from donkeys, coyotes, lynx, and jaguars, to eagles, owls, turkeys, and bats. The Skinwalkers of the Navajo tradition (see pages 119–20) have a similarly wide range of creatures into which they can transform.

Japanese Werefox

In Japan, the story of Kitsune tells of a white fox who transforms into the shape of a woman, marries her lover, and bears several children. Even when her secret is revealed, her husband loves her too much to see her leave, so she spends her nights with him as a woman and her days as a fox.

THE JACKAL-HEADED GOD 

Detail of an Egyptian wall painting showing Anubis with the child pharaoh Tutankhamun. Jackal-headed Anubis is the god of embalming, and he also guides the soul of the deceased into the afterlife.

Wolves & People

The relationship between humans and wolves has been long and complex. Some people love their dogs—which are members of the same species as wolves—with a devotion that leads them to risk their own lives to save the beloved pooch from peril. Other people have hated the animal so much that they have likened it to the Devil. Fortunately, a growing number of people see the wolf for what it is; a wild creature, superbly adapted to its environment, and worthy of respect and conservation.

WOLF ATTACKS

Statistically, we are more likely to be killed by lightning than by a wild wolf: almost all wolf attacks on adult humans are from animals that have been infected with rabies, which sends the creatures mad (see page 45). Although scientific research studying the behavior of *Canis Lupus*, the Gray Wolf, began in earnest in the closing decades of the 20th century, no clear reason has yet been found to explain the wolf's reluctance to prey on human beings.

Child-lifting

There are, however, regular reports of child-lifting, which is when a wolf sneaks into a farm and carries small children away as food. Child-lifting seems to be mostly confined to rural India, where villages exist in close proximity to colonies of wolves whose hunting territory is being built on and taken over by farming.

Competing for resources

It is the age-old bad blood between farmers and wolves that is at the heart of the Hollywood stereotype of the howling-mad murderous wolf. Wolves are very happy to eat sheep and other livestock and, in the farmer's eyes, that makes the wolf a parasitic creature that robs them, taking the food from the mouths of their children.

In ancient Britain, if someone committed a particularly terrible crime they could be condemned as an outlaw. This meant they were outside the protection of the law and could be killed by anyone, anytime, for no reason. From Anglo Saxon times, outlaws such as these were known as called *Wulfes Heafod*—Wolf's head.

Demonizing the wolf

The rise of Christianity made matters much worse for the wolf in the West. Church doctrines spoke of Jesus as the "good shepherd," and of the faithful as his "flock," which meant that the wolf became synonymous with the Devil, who tried to snatch Christian souls and put them into everlasting death. This metaphor vilified the wolf for centuries; a piece of bad press from which it has barely begun to recover.

WOLF DOMESTICATION

No one is sure when wolves first began to be domesticated, but it seems to have occurred in East Asia, and was certainly over 15,000 years

ago. At that time people were beginning to change their lifestyle from one that was as nomadic as the wolves themselves—even competing for the same prey animals—to a more settled hunter–gatherer society. It is ironic that wolves, which have been persecuted for millennia for the protection of domesticated animals, were themselves the very first animals to be domesticated.

THIEF IN THE NIGHT

This woodcut illustration from Jules Verne's novel *P'tit Bonhomme* (1893) shows a hungry wolf stealing baby Jenny (who is soon rescued). The motive here is food, but the reason why wolves adopt human infants is a mystery, although the maternal instinct of the alpha female wolf is highly developed.

Wolf-Children

CROSS-SPECIES ADOPTION

Cases of cross-species nurturing among animals are fairly common, often featuring on TV as light relief at the end of news broadcasts. So there is no reason to reject the idea that other animals may adopt and nurture human young.

Adoptions lasting for a few hours or a day or so have been well-documented, but controversy remains over the authenticity of many, if not all, cases where children have allegedly been raised by non-human animals over a longer time.

Feral television

Wolf children have been popular with authors of fact and fiction alike, and even featured in a TV series aired by ABC between 1977 and 1979. The series was called *Lucan* after the main character (played by Kevin Brophy), and followed the adventures of a man struggling to integrate with human society, having been lost in the woods of Minnesota, USA, as a baby, and found living among the wolves, aged ten.

Hoaxes

There have also been notorious hoaxes, for instance the bestselling book *Surviving with Wolves* (1997). It told of how a young Jewish girl, fleeing the Nazi Holocaust of World War II, was adopted by a wolf pack when she was alone in the woods. Its author, Misha Defonseca, claimed that the book was autobiographical, but it was proved to be fictitious in 2008. Twenty-five real-life cases of children raised by wolves have been cataloged by www.FeralChildren.com, 20 of which occurred in India.

Medieval adoption

The average age of the children when they were found is nine years old, and only three of these children who survived long enough to be found were girls. The earliest recorded case dates to the early 14th century, where a boy who had been taken by wolves at the age of three, was found aged seven in 1304 by Benedictine monks at Hesse, Germany.

Like so many others, the wolf-boy of Hesse after his "rescue" couldn't fully integrate with human society, and preferred his life with the wolves; a recurring theme among many children who spent their early, formative years in this close-knit and intensely physical family group.

INDIAN WOLF-CHILD

Having been lifted by wolves as a baby, Ramu was identified by his parents from birthmarks when he was found—six years later—at Lucknow, India. The calluses on his hands and knees are typical of children raised by wolves.

RADAR

N° 263 - 21 FÉVRIER 1954
Canada 15 cents ★
6 fr. belges - 0 fr. 65 suisses

Hebdomadaire
16 PAGES 30 Francs
Maroc (par avion) 40 fr.

PAGE 2, TOUTE L'HISTOIRE DE

L'ENFANT-LOUP DES INDES

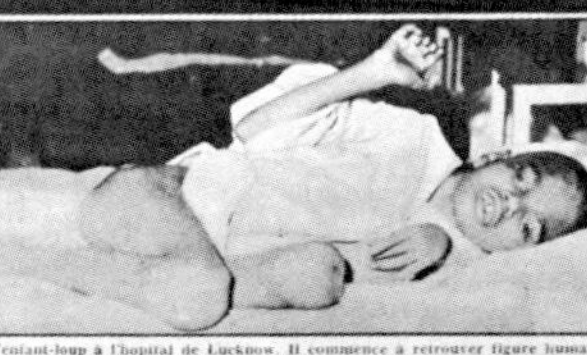

L'enfant-loup à l'hôpital de Lucknow. Il commence à retrouver figure humaine. Les infirmières après l'avoir soigneusement lavé, ont coupé ses longs cheveux.

Indian Adoption

In a unique case in India, a wolf pack adopted two girls. Aged around 18 months and eight years when found, the girls had been adopted at different times and were not sisters. Known as the "Wolf Girls of Midnapore," they were spotted among the wolves in 1920.

A missionary running an orphanage heard a tale of spirits running with a wolf pack through the Bengal jungle. The local people lived in fear of these ghosts, but the missionary built a hide-out from which he could study the den, which was under a massive abandoned termite mound, two stories high.

First the wolves emerged, followed by the two children. Each individual cautiously sniffed the air before loping out of the den into the clearing, running on all-fours. They were clearly human, lithe and healthy, and the hair on their head formed a sort of ball encircling both head and shoulders.

The missionary mustered a hunting party to dig the children out. Two wolves fled into the jungle as the digging began, but the she-wolf protected her offspring fiercely and was shot dead. Two orphaned wolf cubs and both feral children put up a fierce fight, but were eventually hauled out of their den.

The eldest child was given the name Kamala and the infant was called Amala. All their mannerisms were wolfish: they only ate raw meat; they tore away any clothes put on them; they slept in a tight ball; and as they twitched in their dreams, they growled.

Within a year Amala grew ill and died. This was the only time Kamala ever shed tears. It took two years to housetrain her and get her to walk on two feet; a year later she had a vocabulary of around a dozen words. She always longed to return to her wild life, but as a young woman in 1929 she fell ill with kidney failure and died.

THE WOLF-GIRL

The Lobo Wolf Girl of Devil's River (the Lobo is a subspecies, *Canis Lupus Nubilus,* of the ordinary Gray Wolf) was first sighted in San Felipe (Texas, USA) in 1845.

Infrequent sightings

The girl had been taken by Lobo wolves after her mother died in childbirth in 1835, and was next seen ten years later while she was hunting goats with a wolf pack. A year later she was seen again, and she was hunted. After putting up a fierce fight she was captured. Her howling summoned a large pack of wolves, which attacked the local livestock and, in the confusion, the wolf-girl managed to escape. She was seen once more in 1852, when she was aged around 17. She was breast-feeding two cubs on a sandbar in the river and she ran off, carrying the cubs, never to be seen again.

Werewolf Syndrome

WOLFITIS

Werewolf Syndrome, or "Wolfitis," as it is sometimes called, is the common name for some of the many forms of *hypertrichosis,* the condition with excessive hair growth or body hair growing in all the wrong places. Sufferers in the 19th century frequently became well-known as sideshow freaks in circuses and carnivals, with descriptive names such as "dog-man," "wolf-man," "wolf-girl," or simply "werewolf."

Some forms of *hypertrichosis* come about through trauma such as starvation (including *anorexia nervosa*), or drug use, or even some forms of cancer; but Werewolf Syndrome is an inherited condition that people are simply born with and it affects women as much as men.

Pre-birth hair

Before birth, all babies are covered in long, silky, light-colored hair, that usually falls out between the seventh and eighth month of pregnancy. This hair, called "lanugo," remains in *congenital hypertrichosis,* giving the child a furry body, though the palms and soles of the feet remain hairless. In some forms, the fur continues to grow until the baby is at least one year old, and then the hair begins to fall out, leaving the adolescent with a normal pattern of hair (*congenital hypertrichosis lanuginosa*). In another form of the disease the lanugo continues to grow throughout the person's life.

Well-known case

The first documented case of the lifelong form was that of Petrus Gonzales, who was born in the Canary Islands in 1556. He was taken to France as a curiosity, where the nobility patronized him, keeping him in luxury at the French court, enabling him to be educated.

He seemed very intelligent and learned numerous classical and modiern languages thanks to his privileged position. He lived a long life and his children were born with the same medical condition Ambras Syndrome. It was named after the castle of Ambras, where their portraits were exhibited as a novelty. This was where medical science first encountered the family.

Ambras Syndrome

In Ambras Syndrome, hair length of 12 in (30 cm) is not uncommon, and long hair grows on the nose, ears, and even eyelids. The condition is also sometimes associated with facial abnormalities that make those afflicted look even less human, such as extra teeth and a long, prominent nose. In the 19th century, one man was simply known as "Jo-Jo the dog-faced man."

Another, even more extreme form, is *congenital hypertrichosis terminalis,* in which instead of having colorless, silky lanugo, the entire body is permanently covered by the fully pigmented sort of hair that ordinarily only grows on the scalp.

Hirsutism and Porphyria

Hypertrichosis is not the same as being hirsute, which is having hair in the normal places, but too much of it. Hirsutism is particularly noticeable in women who have the condition known a *hyperandrogenism*, which occurs most commonly when the body creates an unusually large quantity of male hormones, resulting in unusual hair growth. The classic fairground sideshow of the Bearded Lady is an example of *hyperandrogenic hirsutism*.

Another medical condition that can cause unusual hair growth is *porphyria*, a term covering at least seven types, each caused by a breakdown in the complex process that produces haem, which enables our bodies to use oxygen. The process is a chain reaction, and a break in one link produces its own unique type of *porphyria*.

Symptoms of *porphyria* include skin sensitivity to light, causing blistering and scarring. In the long term this often leads to skin darkening and excess hair growth. In acute cases, physical symptoms include limb and back pain, muscle cramps, abdominal pain, vomiting, seizures, rapid pulse, and paralysis; while mental symptoms include personality changes, anxiety, paranoia, and hallucinations.

It's easy to imagine *porphyria* being like a typical movie werewolf transformation scene, but not all symptoms occur together, and some only occur in severe cases. Some types of *porphyria* are hereditary, while others are triggered by factors such as drugs and alcohol. A common trigger in women is the change of hormonal balance just before they begin menstruation.

No known cure

The causes of *congenital hypertrichosis* are unknown, but are believed to stem from an inherited disorder, or a spontaneous genetic mutation. There is no known cure for Werewolf Syndrome and at the present time therapy is confined to easing the symptoms through cosmetic treatments such as cutting and shaving the hair, or removing it through chemical

HAIRY ON THE OUTSIDE

Mah-Me was born into the so-called "Hairy Family" of Burma, and was the last of four generations of the family with *congenital hypertrichosis lanuginosa*. She died in the 1880s, aged just 18.

Sufferers Today

There are around 20 cases known to exist in the world today, most of which occur in members of the same family. The Aceves family is from Loreto, Mexico, and traveled with the Mexican National Circus as the "Wolf People."

THE ACEVES FAMILY

Jesus "Chuy" Aceves moved to Los Angeles, California, where he performed in the circus, but despite touring around the world, he became homesick and returned to his family, where he was forced to shave to find a job.

His uncle Manuel, who died recently, was born in 1938 and was the first in the family known to have the condition. Now Chuy is the oldest man in the family with it and one of his two daughters, Karla, has inherited his *hypertrichosis*.

FACING THE WORLD

Despite pressure to conform and shave their all-over, thick, dark hair, the family takes a generally positive view of their condition, believing it to be a blessing from God. However, they have faced verbal and even physical abuse, both in the USA and their native Mexico, from people shocked and ignorant of their circumstances.

Though the "wolf-boys" seem more inclined to accept their hair as it seems curiously attractive to the opposite sex. It is not surprising that the girls, in particular, have taken to shaving in order to attract male companionship and perhaps just to feel "normal." But not all have taken this step—one teenage "wolf-girl" perseveres through her school days with her hair "as nature intended."

epilation, electrolysis, waxing, or, more recently, highly effective laser hair removal. Fortunately, *congenital hypertrichosis* is a very rare condition, so rare that fewer than fifty cases have been securely diagnosed since the Middle Ages. However it is likely that there are many more sufferers who have simply not left their mark in the medical records.

Wolf Girl

The made-for-TV movie *Wolf Girl* (also known as *Blood Moon* and made in 2001) tells the story of Tara Talbot (Victoria Sanchez) who is exhibited in a fictional traveling freak show. Teenage Tara is billed as the "Terrifying Wolf Girl" because of her hypertrichosis, but she just yearns to be normal. This movie is more surreal than screamfest.

Decoding Werewolves

WEREWOLVES AND THE MOON

The Moon, which features in so many stories about werewolves, carries a potent psychological and mythical meaning. The full Moon is literally directly opposite the Sun.

From the werewolf point of view the Sun is warm, bright, familiar, and helps us to see clearly, so the Moon must be chilling, dark, strange, and riddled with evil mysteries. This warped vision dominates much of the werewolf lore arising from medieval Europe, and arose from the same sort of mindset that also saw the duality of good and evil reflected in gender—man and woman.

The sinister moon

The full Moon is powerfully associated with night, dreams, and nightmares. In Shakespeare's time it was believed that the Moon made people depressed and that staring at it for too long could make a person crazy. The word "lunatic" literally means a person who is ruled by the Moon. Each night, while sleeping, we enter a realm over which few of us have any conscious control, and where we are profoundly alone. Here we may come across angels and demons that are conjured up from our hopes and fears, and they are brought to life by the power of our subconscious.

WEREWOLVES IN THE DREAM WORLD

And it is here, in the surreal world of dreams, that we may all experience the forbidden thrills—and their chilling aftermath—of being a werewolf. We don't even have to wait for the night of the full Moon—any night will do. Come to that, even day-dreams work.

While we may revel in the mystery and excitement of feeling the strength and even the pain of the werewolf, such dreams can do a lot more than just entertain us. These dreams can be a window on our mind, if we're brave enough to look into them.

CHANNELING WOLVES

It may be perfectly natural to wish to run with the wolves in dreams, to share the life of the pack, and to know how it is to be a free and powerful: to become a wolf for a while. To promote these dreams, and perhaps to upgrade them into lucid dreams, it's a good idea to study real wolves to learn all about their mannerisms and language. It can be helpful to learn and use the actual body language of the wolf.

It could be useful to keep a diary of significant dreams. This not only helps focus on the dream and get the greatest level of detail recorded straight after waking but also by reading about dreams of years gone by, to see the progress made in "traveling with wolves."

These dreams can give messages that strengthen the spirit, and help people live a more creative

Decoding Dreams

In her book *Dream Decoder* (2006), the author Joules Taylor writes about metamorphosis, and specifically werewolf dreams:

"While just about any creature could be involved in metamorphosis, the wolf is probably the best known, perhaps because of the romance associated with the wolf. The werewolf is a complex image, part victim, part predator. It embodies the idea of becoming something more powerful than yourself in order to enact vengeance on those who have hurt you—but with no accompanying guilt, as the mind becomes animal, acting on instinct. Guilt comes later, as memories of actions taken while occupying wolf form resurface in the human brain. At its most tragic, the werewolf kills its own loved ones. Yet there's a powerful appeal in the idea of being able to borrow an animal's natural skills and experience its life for a time."

While some dream interpretation books provide a uniform "one size fits all" approach, Joules's interpretation of the symbolic werewolf invites us to deepen our understanding of a dream's meaning and message by considering more detailed factors:

"In your dream: Were you a werewolf or did you meet one? What feelings were associated with the dream—do you feel yourself to be a victim in your waking life or do you fantasize about getting your own back on those who have hurt you, in a form that leaves the human you blameless?" The answers to these questions increase our understanding of the way the mind is working, and can also help us recognize and sort out problems we are facing in our lives. Getting to grips with nightly dreams can even inspire greater self-confidence, help us spot and seize opportunities, and bring us closer to those other dreams—the hopes and ambitions we all cherish.

Science and psychology teach us that we are only consciously aware of a small fraction of the information we take in. When we dream, our subconscious mind lets us know what else we have taken in without noticing. Dreams do more than offer us something to think about; they are an escape from the strictures of day-to-day life. We can achieve a freedom that is impossible in reality, and it is entirely right to enjoy exploring a dreamscape just as we would a holiday destination. This lack of restrictions deserves to be relished for its own sake.

The Threat of Rabies

It has been suggested that the common theme of people being infected by a werewolf when it bites them is actually folklore reacting to the very real threat of rabies.

The main way in which people contract the disease rabies is by being bitten by an infected and maddened animal. Very often they are bitten by a dog that has contracted the virus from a wild animal, and has been driven out of its mind by the virus until it behaves with extraordinary aggression and savagery, like a "demonic" wolf.

The most common early symptoms in humans are anxiety, disorientation, and a yearning to be left alone somewhere peaceful, quiet, warm, and away from bright lights—a snug den would be perfect. Then comes an overwhelming fear of swallowing and a corresponding phobia of water. Delirium quickly follows, with hallucinations and raving that often includes attacking and biting others.

To make matters worse for the patient, these attacks of manic behavior are interspersed with periods of mental lucidity. At these times the sufferer is painfully aware of their uncontrollable outbursts, and aware of their condition—half human, half beast.

The way most werewolves infect people is by biting at their throat, which is also the point of attack by which the rabies virus reaches the brain and affects the victim most rapidly. If left untreated, rabies is usually fatal.

and fulfilling life. Psychologists say that dreams are a way of engaging in a dialog with the self. That dialog is vital, and the insights received are real and precious.

SHAMANIC TRADITIONS

Another way of contacting these inner secrets is through Shamanic ritual. These ceremonies are often long and exhausting, and many create trance-like states in which the ties that bind the practitioner's spirit to their body are loosened. Their liberated spirit may travel into the "otherworld" in the form of a personal totem animal, such as a wolf, for example.

Shamans can also practice another form of beneficial "werewolfism," in which they invoke the spirit of the wolf to "possess" their body. They believe that this gives them the creature's physical powers of strength and stamina. This idea may

underlie some Native American traditions, such as the Skinwalker (see pages 119–20), although popular culture favors a different interpretation.

SHAMANIC WOLVES IN ANCIENT TIMES

Herodotus (484–418 BCE) is regarded as the earliest Greek historian, and he records in his *History* a snippet of werewolf lore. He says that every person in the Neuri tribe (which then occupied a territory now in the region of Belarus and Eastern Poland), transforms into a wolf for several days each year. Afterward they simply revert to their usual form.

Herodotus firmly states that he thinks this is impossible, but he also stresses the seriousness with which the belief is declared by both the neighboring tribe of Scythians and by Greeks living there. It seems likely that the Neurian claim refers to some sort of shamanic ritual that feels absolutely real to the person involved, but is not the physical transformation Herodotus assumed they meant. Words can conjure very different ideas in the minds of people with different ways of thinking.

NATIVE AMERICAN NOOTKA MASK 

A fearsome wolf mask used for ritual purposes to invoke the spirit of the wolf. This is worn by a member of one of the First Nations, the Nuu-chah-nulth (Nootka) people, whose traditional territory is on the west of Vancouver Island, Canada.

Werewolves, Wolves, & Drugs

Sometimes, werewolf dreams creep over the threshold of consciousness and stream into the waking world—either through the madness of werewolfism ("lycanthropy"), or through another sort of chemical imbalance in the brain: hallucinogenic drugs.

A shamanic practitioner will have had many years of serious education in the powers of psychoactive drugs, and will have mastered techniques of directing the experience to gain knowledge. In contrast, a recreational drug-user may literally "blow" their own mind, producing a powerful but essentially meaningless trip, which they could find very scary. But at least they will know it was "just" the effect of the drug.

ACCIDENTAL DRUG USE

Imagine if a potent hallucinogen was inadvertently mixed into something you'd never suspect, like your everyday bread: suddenly your world turns upside down—you can see all the figments of your dreams are walking around in broad daylight—and seeing is believing. If everyone around you has the same contaminated food, it will be the same for them—the boundary separating waking life from the world of dreams and nightmares has simply dissolved.

MEDIEVAL HYSTERIA

Ergot poisoning, caused by a small fungus that grows on rye, which was ground into flour and baked into bread, was common in the Middle Ages. Coincidentally perhaps, its shape has given it the name *Wolfszahn*—Wolf-tooth. Ergot has both the hallucinogenic properties of LSD and severely painful side-effects (guaranteeing a "bad trip").

It is thought to be a likely cause of much of the hysteria that periodically plagued Europe and northern America, with tales of witches, possession by devils, and transformations into werewolves. An outbreak of this fungus in the village granary could infect the whole village's daily bread, and with no idea what was causing the "magic," the villagers could continue using the grain, suffering from the poisoning, until the next harvest.

What we can now explain in terms of neurotoxins would seem like an outbreak of magic to our forebears, but it underlines the fact that, without a healthy mental balance between our conscious and subconscious—the sun and the moon, day and night—we may all fall prey to the lures of extreme and dangerous beliefs.

The Strength of Werewolves

Apart from its physical appearance and emotional character, the werewolf is renowned for its superhuman strength. This monstrous muscular power is frequently channeled by its sheer aggression, turning the angry werewolf into a truly terrifying beast. When this brutal energy is unleashed and directed at a physically weaker person, such as a young woman, for example, the result can be lethal.

But a surge of physical strength accompanied by emotional rage (or fear) is something natural and possible in every human being. *Epinephrine* (adrenaline) is a hormone whose release is triggered by the basic fight-or-flight instinct, and it provides extraordinary and immediate physical abilities. It can make us run faster than we ever thought possible, or it can make us able to launch into a fight with greater strength combined with an immunity to feeling pain.

THE USES OF ADRENALINE

Released from the adrenal glands, situated on the top of our kidneys, this primal survival kit boosts the supply of oxygen and glucose to our muscles and brain. As well as enhancing our muscular performance at times of crisis, along with norepinephrine (which is also released at moments of extreme stress), epinephrine acts to sharpen our mind. We can see, hear, smell, and feel in much greater detail. We can think and react so quickly, and our senses are so intensely alive, it is as if time slows down for us (it's a "Matrix moment") in a state of heightened awareness. We are lifted, for just a little while, outside of our normal consciousness, and we are momentarily more than human.

An addictive high

Designed for emergency situations, such as evading predators or seizing prey, we aren't supposed to encounter circumstances that trigger the release of adrenaline very often in our lives. Adrenaline junkies, however, enjoy the heightened sense of awareness that epinephrine provides so much that they continually push the boundaries of personal safety in their attempts to recapture the extraordinary feeling of the "adrenaline rush"—hence the popularity of so-called "extreme" sports. Of course, after the natural high wears off, there is inevitably a corresponding natural depression, in which mind and body struggle to make the adjustment to normality.

WEREWOLVES CLASH →

The transformed werewolf can easily overcome an untransformed opponent. Here the transformed Dr. Wilfred Glendon (right) attacks the untransformed werewolf that had originally bitten him, infecting him with the curse (*Werewolf of London*, 1935).

WEREWOLF OF LONDON
RE-RELEASE

The CURSE OF THE
WEREWOLF
in Eastman COLOR
Starring CLIFFORD EVANS · OLIVER REED · YVONNE ROMAIN · CATHERINE FELLER
Screenplay by JOHN ELDER Directed by TERENCE FISHER Produced by ANTHONY HINDS Executive Producer MICHAEL CARRERAS
A HAMMER FILM PRODUCTION · A UNIVERSAL-INTERNATIONAL RELEASE

Chapter 2

Werewolves & Popular Culture

Werewolves in Movies

THE APPEAL OF THE MALE WEREWOLF

The great majority of werewolves we read about or watch in movies are male. There seems to be something about the raw physical aggression of the transformed werewolf that makes us assume it must be masculine. It's certainly true that when a wolf-man makes an entrance he can expect to be center-stage. With shaggy fur, long claws, aggressive stance, and blood on his muzzle, the werewolf is going to draw the eye and command respect. Or else. Usually in movies that's the moment when everybody starts screaming and running; always a bad move. It's canine instinct to chase and try to catch anything that runs.

The trapped man

But sometimes in these tales there's one person in the crowd who doesn't scream and doesn't run. Someone who can see beyond the bloodlust in the werewolf's eyes, to see the soul of the man trapped inside the wolf. Usually, this special individual is his lover, and many tales about werewolves are really love stories. The earliest movies focused on the tragic romance of the doomed relationship between werewolf and heroine, but audiences grew over-familiar with this storyline and wanted something more shocking. Brutal gore-fests delighted audiences in the 1980s, as teenagers explored extremes of random on-screen violence. But interest in these excesses has turned full circle, and the bloodthirsty beasts of the big screen are beginning to give way to increasingly well-groomed, almost "metrosexual," werewolves. Werewolves in popular culture are now willing to discover their sensitive sides once again.

WHY MALE?

The ideas behind this stereotype are complex and some of the assumptions controversial, but as most early writers of werewolf stories were men, perhaps an element of male pride played a part. For a man who believes he was created in the image of an almighty God, it would be embarrassing to be defeated and devoured by a female—of any species. Such a man regards it as his divine duty to fight and overcome other men. Each time he is successful, he increases his status in society and rises closer to the top—closer to godhead—eventually to become the alpha male. Or so the theory goes. This behavior in the human male clearly mirrors lupine nature remarkably closely and reinforces the male–wolf link.

LOVE OR LUST?

The scary werewolf and the woman in the red dress are classic icons of the genre. Here in *The Wolf Man* (1941) animal passions have broken the bounds of social intercourse, and imperiled the heroine—and there will be a heavy price to be paid.

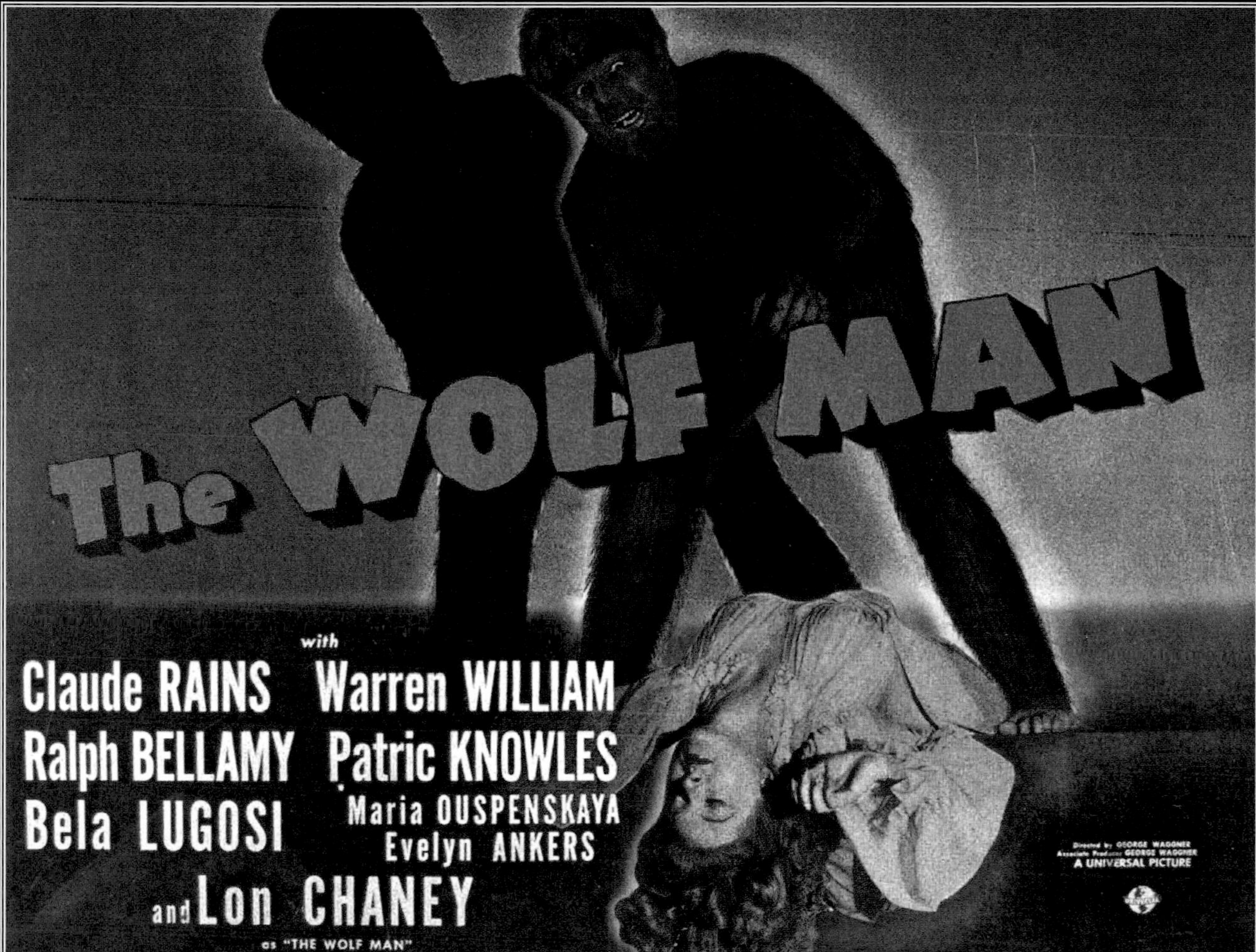

The WOLF MAN
with
Claude RAINS
Warren WILLIAM
Ralph BELLAMY
Patric KNOWLES
Bela LUGOSI
Maria OUSPENSKAYA
Evelyn ANKERS
and Lon CHANEY
as "THE WOLF MAN"
A UNIVERSAL PICTURE

NO GIRLS ALLOWED

It would be a terrible blow to the male ego to be eaten by a woman, even if she had turned a bit beastly. It would be humiliating, which would literally add insult to injury. For the early writers it simply wouldn't do, particularly as most readers of werewolf literature were male. Such a storyline would make them cringe. Worse, it could be viewed as subversive, almost blasphemous in its attempt to turn its god-given natural order upside down. Women defeating men? Unthinkable!

Male-centric

Ironically, this male-centric view of reality, with its inflexible sense of self-righteousness, could be seen as the "dark side" of masculinity. The lust for power and the constant threat of inflicting bodily harm on anyone who dares challenge his dominance, are hallmarks of "the beast" in man.

The werewolf is the embodiment of brute force coupled with human ingenuity and the raw cunning of a madman. He is the savage pack animal that is not controlled by the civilizing aspects of humanity.

IT'S A MAN THING

The movie *Underworld: Rise of the Lycans* (2009) charts the evolution of the Lycans—from brutal werewolves that cannot revert to human form, to humane Lycans who can transform at will. Such self-mastery mirrors every man's inner journey.

The Tyrant Wolf

Extreme selfishness, coupled with ruthlessness, create a monster—a tyrant. Every day we can see tyranny raging throughout the world, from political leaders that care more about their own wealth than the wellbeing of their people, to the drunken father who terrorizes his children.

POLITICAL TYRANTS

Tyranny is nothing new. The classical Greek philosopher Plato tried to find a way to stop predatory people from succeeding in politics.

In his work *The Republic* he recorded his thoughts in a fictional discussion that is still relevant today in its description of the way power breeds corruption. Significantly, he used the werewolf as an example of the extreme tyrant.

The tyrant of Arcadia

In this discussion he refers to Lycaon, the tyrant of Arcadia, who allegedly devoured a baby he killed as a sacrifice to the god Zeus Lycaeus (see page 134). The only cure Plato suggests for such an inhumane tyrant is that he should be slain like a wild beast.

The tyrant is the epitome of the werewolf that cannot return to human form, but is doomed by its bloodthirsty nature to remain a beast forever. The killing, or extermination, of such vile monsters remains a popular theme with modern authors and movie-makers.

Socrates

According to Plato, fellow philosopher Socrates explains about tyranny using the wolf/ Lycaeus metaphor, explaining that democracy may transform into tyranny (in a way that is comparable to the human–wolf transformation). Here is a selection from Socrates's words in *The Republic*:

"The people select a political champion and support him, giving him a position of power in the government. How does he grow to become a tyrant? Surely it follows the course of the transformation told about the temple of Zeus Lycaeus in Arcadia. The tale that says any man who devours part of a human being is doomed to become a wolf. The people's champion is like that man. Emboldened by his popularity, he can make false allegations so the justice system commits murder for him—by executing anyone he wants killed. With his lying tongue and lips he tastes the blood of his fellow citizens. After this, what will be his destiny? Surely he will either perish at the hands of his enemies, or else he will change from a man to a wolf—that is, he will become a tyrant."

Underworld

The *Underworld* series of movies is unusual in featuring a vicious werewolf that cannot transform back into human form. This werewolf is so completely bestial in its behavior that eradicating the whole species seems the only safe way of dealing with it. However, even from this bleak premise, the writers find a way to evolve this werewolf to become a creature that successfully combines the strength of the beast with the heart of a man.

In this way, *Underworld* presents us with an explosive mixture of the two eternal themes—death and love—themes that are interwoven in almost every werewolf story. It also features a war between two of the best-loved monsters about.

The third movie *Underworld: Rise of the Lycans* (released 2009), is set in medieval Europe, and is a prequel to the others, which are set in modern times. This third movie is an origin myth explaining how the werewolf clan began.

The word "Lycan" is an abbreviation of Lycanthrope, meaning wolf-man, and is used to refer to the Lycans, who are werewolves by another name.

THE UNDERWORLD STORY

According to the *Underworld* movies, in the 5th century, Hungarian warlord Alexander Corvinus is infected by a plague that kills most people, but uniquely, it makes him immortal.

Alexander Corvinus fathers twin sons, William and Markus, who both carry the immortality gene. When William is bitten by a wolf, he transforms into a wolf, becoming the first Lycan.

When Markus is bitten by a bat he becomes a vampire. Alexander has another child, a mortal, who carries a dormant copy of the plague virus, but who possesses no special abilities.

Spread of mutations

William, the first Lycan, is unable to return to human form. He and the Lycans he makes are monstrous, ultra-savage animals. The twins' mutations are infectious and easily spread by biting. Soon great numbers of immortal werewolves and vampires exist alongside humanity, secretly, in the "Underworld."

The vampires seek to exterminate the werewolves and, in this role, they are the protectors of civilization and champions of weaker individuals. In 1202, the eldest and strongest Lycan, William, is captured and imprisoned, supposedly for all time.

Lucian rises

However, not all the wild Lycans are killed. Some are kept alive and enslaved by the vampires as guard dogs to protect them while they sleep through the perilous daylight hours. This state of affairs settles into a relationship that appears to be set in stone. But appearances can be deceptive.

A Lycan arises who is able to transform from the wolf state back to human form. Lucian is the first of this "second generation" of Lycans. He and his followers become increasingly civilized and far less furry than their ancestors. However, they are still enslaved.

Physical strength

Like all werewolves, the Lycans are incredibly strong and can easily kill vampires in hand to hand—or tooth to fang—combat. It is only the vampires' superior intellect and organizational skills that enable them to dominate the Lycans so completely during the early centuries.

Transformation

That situation changes, however, when Lucian learns to transform back again; a process he passes on to the second generation of Lycans. To begin with, their transformation back into the wolf form is only possible during the time of the full Moon, but eventually even this obstacle is overcome and the Lycans are able to transform whenever they need to.

Like vampires, Lycans don't age, so they are immortal unless they are slain. William, the first-ever Lycan, survives his imprisonment for over eight hundred years, with neither food nor water, and is merely weakened by the ordeal.

The Hybrid

The *Underworld* movies dramatically redefine the traditional relationship between werewolf and vampire in the compelling idea of the Hybrid—a genetically merged creature that combines the abilities of both creatures into a being more powerful than either. In particular, the Lycans want the Hybrid to be powerful enough that it will enable them to defeat their ages-old enemies: the vampires.

Enhanced senses

Lycans possess enhanced senses of smell, sight, and hearing, and they also have an extrasensory ability to detect the proximity of a vampire. When the Lycans become Hybrids their sensory powers are enormously boosted. The origin of the Lycans was a fluke genetic mutation—a random change in their DNA—so their condition was inherited, rather than self-induced, and they simply cannot help themselves.

A NEW BREED OF LYCAN

Lucian (Michael Sheen) in the movie *Underworld* (2003) has waged a guerrilla war for centuries against the cruel tyrants that slew his true love for the crime of loving him. He was the first Lycan to master the art of transformation.

The Monster Club

The notion of the Hybrid monster is not new. A fine example is offered in the novel *The Monster Club* (1975) by Ronald Chetwynd-Hayes.

As the title suggests, this is not in the same vein as *Underworld,* but it does have its serious side. The baby werevamp, born to doting parents George (a werewolf) and Carola (vampire), is soon made an orphan through the efforts of the local vicar.

Fortunately the werevamp, Manfred, can take care of himself, and grows to become a member in good standing of the club, in Swallow Street, London, UK.

ALIEN WEREWOLVES

Lycans and vampires are genetic mutations and so is the werewolf that appears in the acclaimed British TV series *Doctor Who.* Aired in 2006, though set in 1879, the second episode of the second series was entitled *Tooth and Claw,* and featured an alien intelligence that fell to Earth and adapted itself to live in a succession of human hosts, turning them into werewolves.

LOVING THE ENEMY

Selene (Kate Beckinsale) in the movie *Underworld* (2003) is a Death Dealer devoted to exterminating all Lycans. Her life is beautifully simple until she meets a man infected by the Lycans (and doomed to become one of them)... She falls in love with him.

Establishing the Empire

The bloodthirsty creature is nurtured by a secretive order of monks, who control it by using its dislike of mistletoe. Seduced by supernatural mystery, the monks assist it in its endeavor to establish the Empire of the Wolf.

They lure Queen Victoria to their sanctuary so the beast can bite her and, in doing so, pass itself into her body and rule the British Empire through her.

Excess

While moonlight gives the alien werewolf creature strength, the Doctor realizes that an excess of moonlight could harm it.

He uses a specially adapted telescope to focus the light of the full Moon onto the creature. This beam, when further amplified by a large diamond, destroys the alien and saves the Earth from a new and immortal tyrant.

SKINWALKERS

The same can be said of the werewolves in the Canadian movie *Skinwalkers* (2007), but there is a difference. Whereas the Lycans evolved into a civilized form of werewolf, leaving their tyrannical ancestors behind, the Skinwalkers evolved into two packs who exist alongside each other: one predatory, aggressive, and oppressive, and the other altruistic, peaceful, and social.

Good Skinwalkers

This movie attempts to bring the ancient Native American lore of the Navajo Skinwalker, the man-wolf, up to date. The story is only loosely based on the true tradition, though. For instance, it features good Skinwalkers and as we shall see (see page 119) the traditional tales insist that there is really no such thing as a good Skinwalker.

The film has plenty of evil Skinwalkers, who arrive as a motorcycle gang easily identifiable by their counter-culture clothing and habit of killing people. They are young, good-looking, strong, and intensely proud that they are not merely human. Their problem is that they have fed on human flesh, which is absolutely addictive. They believe themselves to be a superior breed and, as such, are the vanguard of the master race, the overlords who will treat ordinary people as food. In this sense, these Skinwalkers are clearly the modern incarnation of the tyrants of classical Arcadia.

Confrontation

The movie's action revolves around the confrontation between the two sorts of Skinwalkers, making it a classic battle between good and evil. Caught in the middle, is a 12-year-old boy called Timothy (Matthew Knight). Although Timothy doesn't know it, he is the subject of a prophecy—the "Rise of the Red Moon"—and it is this prophecy that has brought the evil Skinwalkers to his sleepy little home town inhabited by good skinwalkers.

The creation of Skinwalkers

All the Skinwalkers, both good and bad, were thought to be born without the "gene that separates human from animal." That genetic mutation explains how they can switch forms. The evil Skinwalkers revel in their ability to transform and want to maintain their lifestyle, which capitalizes on physical strength.

On the other hand, the good skinwalkers reject bloodlust and frenzied slaughter, and nurture moral strength instead. Timothy's blood holds the cure to all Skinwalkers. When he turns 13 years old (and it's nearly his birthday), his blood will mature and have the miraculous power to regenerate the Skinwalkers' defective gene and reverse its effects, making them completely human. The good Skinwalkers have nurtured this hope since the prophecy was first made. If they can keep the boy alive, he will cure them.

Bloody conflict

The conflict is blood-soaked and gory and, in its uncut version, not the sort of thing a youngster like Timothy should watch. The movie concludes with the child savior embarking on a mission to distribute his healing blood to anyone who is in need of it. He also injects it into bullets, to distribute into the body of any Skinwalker that doesn't voluntarily recognize the potential of a human lifestyle. By having the good Skinwalkers unite and take up arms against the bad ones, this movie offers a satisfying take on the theme of the common people working together to defeat the evil, tyrannical Skinwalkers, which is especially pleasing because we get to see two types of werewolf for the price of one!

FIGHTING FOR THE FUTURE

In the movie *Skinwalkers* (2007) the conflict between good and evil is focused on an innocent child. Timothy (Matthew Knight) and his mother (Rhona Mitra) must escape the sub-human werewolf pack that wants him dead.

Revolt Against Repression

THE HOWLING

We have seen the Lycans revolt against the vampires' regime, but another famous movie that portrays the results of psychological repression in werewolves is *The Howling* (1981).

Setting the standard

Both a classic and a cult movie, the first in *The Howling* series set the standard for just about every werewolf movie that followed. Though the plot now seems predictable, at the time it was an original concept. TV reporter Karen White (Dee Wallace) is being stalked by serial killer Eddie Quist (Robert Picardo). While helping the police catch him, she is attacked, but the police intervene and kill him.

The legacy

Karen suffers amnesia afterward, and suffers from recurring nightmares, so her doctor, Dr. Waggner (Patrick Macnee), sends her to The Colony—a retreat he runs for special patients. Only, as she finds out later, all the other "patients" are vicious and malevolent werewolves. Dr. Waggner insists that the werewolves should coexist with humans—particularly by not eating them. But his patients are reluctant to eat only animals. The werewolves are starting to rebel against him and his ideals. These werewolves can change at will, not needing the Moon to effect the transformation, but silver is the only thing that can permanently kill them. If they're "killed" by any other means they regenerate and come back to life in three days.

Repressing healthy emotions is rarely effective for long, as their energy tends to find release in another form—often destructively. However, care needs to be taken when removing mental blocks that inhibit behavior, because like an uncorked champagne bottle spraying everyone with effervescence, the sufferer may immediately lurch to the other extreme. In this psychological thriller, the werewolves erupt in an orgy of killing.

> "Repression is the father of neurosis, of self-hatred... We should never try to deny the beast, the animal within us."
>
> Dr. Waggner, *The Howling*

UNLEASHED PASSION

The nymphomaniac Marsha (Elisabeth Brooks) is the uninhibited alpha female of the werewolf pack in *The Howling* (movie, 1981). She is the sister of serial killer Eddie, and is the only werewolf left alive at the end of the movie.

The Divided Self

MULTIPLE PERSONALITIES

There is a psychological condition called "multiple personality disorder" (now known as dissociative identity disorder), where two or more personalities occupy a single mind. The famous story by Robert Louis Stevenson of *The Strange Case of Dr Jekyll and Mr Hyde* (1886) presents a case in point.

Jekyll and Hyde

The story that coined the phrase "Jekyll and Hyde," meaning two opposite personalities present in one individual, was inspired by a dream. The plot revolves around a scientist—Dr Jekyll—who develops a potion separating the evil side of his character from his good side. He had hoped that the evil side would disappear, leaving him wholly good, but instead he transorms into two distinct people—a split personality—with Mr Hyde gaining the upper hand.

Fighting for control

In a split personality, it is as though there is more than one person inhabiting the single body, often fighting for control. In the same way, the werewolf has to contain the two personalities of its violent, hungry animal self and its civilized, human self. The human self does not want to hurt people or ruin the normal life which it enjoys, therefore the werewolf's mind is forever at war with itself—with two distinct personalities fighting for dominance.

SILVER BULLET

The movie *Silver Bullet* (1985, screenplay by Stephen King, based on his own book *Cycle of the Werewolf*, 1983) features a Baptist minister who is also a werewolf, and embarks on a killing spree each month.

Role inversion

Back in human form, the Reverend Lowe (Everett McGill) self-righteously justifies his secret atrocities by considering how sinful his victims were. Such a complete inversion of roles—from savior to psychopath—was unthinkable to the people of the small town in Maine, USA, for a long time, so the Reverend escaped suspicion.

Eventually it is a young boy who first raises the alarm and stops the Reverend's reign of terror. This idea of the good and bad self is also exploited in the werewolf lifestyle depicted in the adventure movie *Dog Soldiers* (2002).

THIS IS NOT PUPPY LOVE

The movie *Dog Soldiers* shows what happens when vicious werewolves meet professional soldiers in close-quarter combat. But in their human phase, these werewolves are people you'd be happy to have living next door.

FROM THE PRODUCER OF HELLRAISER

SEAN PERTWEE
LIAM CUNNINGHAM
KEVIN McKIDD

DOG SOLDIERS

SIX SOLDIERS
FULL MOON
NO CHANCE.

Dog Soldiers Plot

Set in Scotland, the film opens with two young campers enjoying a peaceful holiday evening by the campfire—under a full Moon. The woman presents her partner with a solid-silver letter opener. Suddenly something pulls open the zip of their tent, drags her outside, and then viciously attacks her.

The scene switches to a soldier, Cooper, running through a wood, trying to escape the men and dogs hunting him. He is caught, but the leader of the hunters—Captain Ryan—congratulates him for evading capture for so long. Cooper fails his final test when he refuses to shoot one of the dogs, despite it being a direct order from the Captain.

A month later Sergeant Wells and his squad, Cooper among them, are air-lifted into a Scottish wood on a training exercise. This squad of dedicated soldiers on a training exercise are led by a flare to the site of another army camp, where they find equipment, blood, and guts (literally), but no bodies. One man, Captain Ryan, is left alive, and he has been seriously clawed. He's in shock, and as they try to help him he says, over and over again, "There was only supposed to be one..." The soldiers are attacked by monstrous creatures. Sergeant Wells is clawed and almost disemboweled, but the squad manages to escape, dragging their wounded companions with them. They are met by a zoologist named Megan, who drives them to a farmhouse.

At the farmhouse the soldiers discover that their attackers are werewolves. As the night progresses, and their ammunition diminishes, the creatures make greater inroads into the farmhouse. The soldiers also discover that Ryan and his men had been sent to capture one of the werewolves for the Special Weapons Division—and that their squad were the bait. The werewolves are vicious, tough killers; their bodies are human and their heads elegantly wolf-like. Despite this, they do retain some human intelligence: they know how to disable Megan's car.

The twist, however, is that the werewolves are the owners of the farmhouse and in their human form they are kind and gentle people. Another twist is that Megan herself is a werewolf and has been resisting the transformation in order to bring the soldiers to the house. They kill her as she transforms. Bullets have no effect on these werewolves—only decapitation works. Silver makes the most effective weapon, but that is in rather short supply in a werewolf's home.

The Power of Love

THE BONDS OF INFATUATION

Although love can be the ultimate healing force, the most obvious and vivid example of our inner struggle is the one that arises when the fiery bonds of infatuation snare our hearts.

Threatening urges

When we become infatuated, the urges of jealousy, pride, dominance, and control can all rear up like a ravenous werewolf pack and start tearing away at the person we thought we were. These forces threaten to tear us apart and can drag us down very low indeed, and we must fight to overcome their destructive influence. Surrender is not an option—to give into these negative impulses is to become a monster like the werewolf permanently in its wolf form.

There is only one hope for such a dangerous creature: to escape being ostracized and cast out from the companionship of friends, we must undergo a further transformation. We have to transform back into human form. How? It is important to submit to the power of love and embrace the idea of self-sacrifice.

Emotionally violent

Our personal emotional battles inevitably spill out sometimes and hurt the very people we love, and when this happens we must be humble enough to accept their forgiveness. For a werewolf returning to his human form, the discovery of the hurt he has caused in wolf form can be almost unbearable.

A mirror

The werewolf's condition is extreme, and the transformation depicted with dreamlike symbolism, but as with a dream, we understand the meaning of the message he brings. And it hurts. We recognize our own heartache in the suffering he endures—he is a mirror to our soul.

THE WOLF MAN

It was love, fate, and the tragic infliction of a werewolf's bite that gripped audiences in 1941 when Universal Pictures released *The Wolf Man.* This classic movie established the look and feel of the werewolf in the hearts of cinema-goers for a generation.

The working title of the movie was *Destiny,* and the hand of fate certainly features in the plot. Threads of primal folklore and modern psychology mix to give the movie visceral thrills and intellectual bite; but it is the romantic tension between the hero and heroine—an illicit love that offers them a life above and beyond their dreams —that really captures the audience and holds them spellbound.

The son returns

Set in a sleepy British village one misty autumn, the plot begins when the estranged son of the

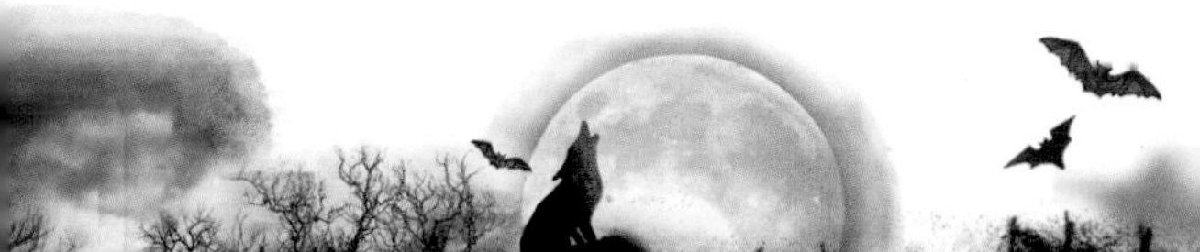

Lord of Talbot Castle returns to visit his father. Larry Talbot (Lon Chaney Jr.), who is a self-made and practical man, has barely settled in when he sees and falls for Gwen (Evelyn Ankers), the daughter of the owner of the local antiques shop.

Silver handle

They first meet when Larry calls at the shop. He finds an old walking stick with a heavy silver handle shaped like the head of a wolf. There is an additional ornament on the wolf's head: a flat circle containing a five-pointed star.

As he buys it Gwen explains that the symbol is a pentagram, the mark of the werewolf, and that the werewolf sees it on the hand of his next victim. Larry makes a humorous quip about wolves, and Gwen points out, in all seriousness, that the fairytale of *Little Red Riding Hood* is actually a werewolf story.

The Prophecy

Gwen quotes an old gypsy rhyme that has become famous among werewolf aficionados: "Even a man who is pure in heart and says his prayers by night, may become a wolf when the wolfsbane blooms and the Autumn Moon is bright."

Gypsies are camping near by, and despite being engaged to one of the Castle's staff, Gwen goes with Larry to have their fortunes told. On the way Gwen's friend Jenny (Fay Helm) picks some wolfsbane flowers. Gwen and Larry wander off, flirting a little, while Jenny goes to have her fortune told.

The symbol

Bela the fortune teller (Bela Lugosi) throws aside Jenny's wolfsbane blooms, but offers to read her hand. There, in her palm he sees the symbol of the star inside the circle—the pentagram. He orders her to leave immediately, and she runs out.

As they walk through the woods Gwen and Larry hear the howl of a wolf, and then suddenly a woman's screams pierce the night. Larry runs through the mist toward the sound and sees a wolf attacking Jenny. He enters the fray and is savagely bitten before he kills the creature with his silver-headed stick.

Mistaken identity

In the morning, Larry visits Gwen at the antiques shop, where he is confronted by Jenny's mother and a crowd of her friends, who accuse him of being responsible for the girl's death. They point out the immorality of Gwen being out with him when she is engaged to another man. Also as heir to the ancient aristocratic legacy of Talbot Castle, they consider Larry's affair with Gwen to be a mere dalliance with a social inferior.

WILL HE? WON'T HE? 

The moment of truth in *The Wolf Man* (1941). The werewolf (Lon Chaney Jr.) finds his true love Gwen (Evelyn Ankers) alone in the Moonlight, and she faints in his arms. He is torn between bloodlust and love.

Rather than sympathize over their bereavement, Larry behaves as though his inner wolf is breaking loose and becomes angry, frightening them out of the shop. That night, Larry stumbles across an old gypsy woman called Maleva (played by Maria Ouspenskaya), who tells him that Bela has been a werewolf, and that now, Larry is one, too. She presents him with a charm, a pentagram pendant, for protection.

Protection

Larry meets Gwen and tells her he is a werewolf. He gives her the gypsy's protective charm, but she feels unable to accept the gift from him, as it could be construed to be a lover's token, and says she will pay him for it. As she hunts for a penny, he steals a kiss. She feels this is too much too soon, and hurries away, distraught.

Transformation

That night Larry's body grows hairy, until he is covered from head to foot with fur. Transformed into the wolf man he strides into the night, killing a gravedigger.

The police track the paw prints of a wolf that are all around the body, which lead directly to Talbot Castle. They want to interrogate Larry, but his doctor intervenes; explaining that clearly Larry is raving when he talks about werewolves.

All in the mind

Larry's father, Sir John (Claude Rains), describes werewolfism as a form of schizophrenia based on the good and evil that resides in every man's soul. He dismisses such crude black and white interpretations, preferring, instead, the many shades of gray. The doctor adds his opinion that a man who is lost in the maze of his mind can imagine himself to be anything. Larry seizes on the idea that mental suggestion and self hypnosis could make a man believe he's a werewolf. Perhaps it's just his imagination after all.

Caught in a trap

That night Larry finds himself in the woods, his ankle caught in the metal jaws of a wolf-trap. Maleva is standing over him—she has just recited a solemn chant that transformed him back into human form. He flees back to the village, and tosses small stones against Gwen's window. She wakes and races downstairs to let him in. Panicking, he declares himself a werewolf, and says he must leave at once. Gwen says they can leave immediately, but he refuses to take her. His overriding desire is to protect the girl he loves—from himself.

Pentagram

Gwen shows Larry that she is wearing the protective pendant, but this glimmer of hope dies

BATTLE OF THE (SCREEN) GIANTS 

Having discovered silver bullets can't actually kill him, the Wolf Man (Lon Chaney Jr.) travels to Frankenstein's castle to find the secrets of life that will enable him to die. The monster (Bela Lugosi) fights the werewolf in the final reel of *Frankenstein Meets the Wolf Man* (1943).

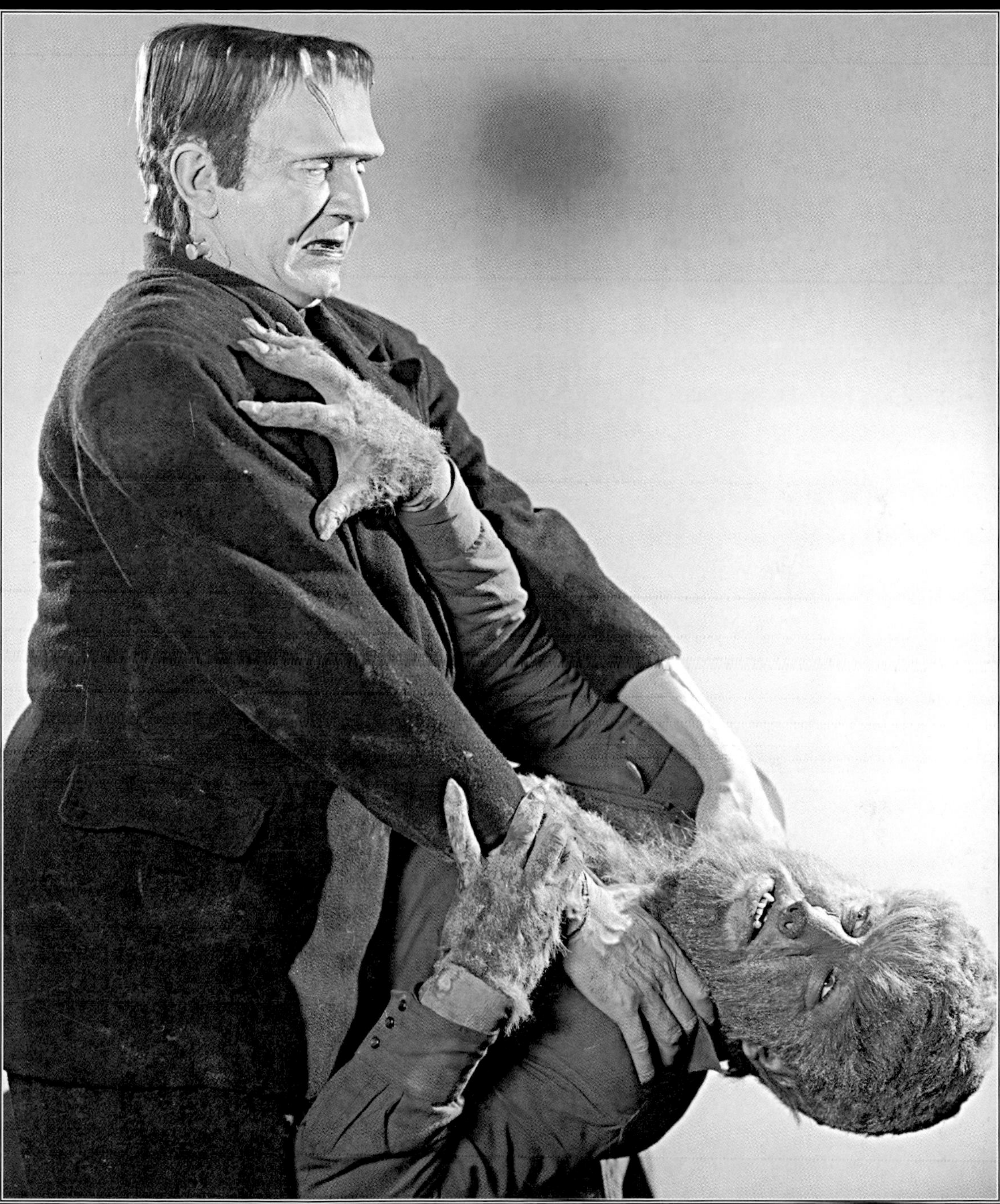

when Larry sees the shadowy mark of the pentagram on her palm. He tears himself away from her and charges off into the darkness.

Good and evil

Briefly returning to the Castle to collect the essentials for his escape, Larry meets his father, who convinces him to stay and face his fear. Sir John believes the werewolfism is wholly in Larry's mind and locks him in his room for his own safety. When Sir John announces he must leave, Larry insists he takes the antique stick with the heavy silver handle. The hunters are vigilant and, as a volley of shots ring out, they claim to have shot the wolf man twice, but that didn't stop it. Someone suggests that they should have used silver bullets.

The final pounce

Gwen is also out in the woods, looking for Larry, and the wolf man sees her. For a very brief moment there is the hope that he will recognize her and they will find safety together. But he growls, steps forward, and pounces. As the horror grips her, Gwen screams. Sir John is first on the

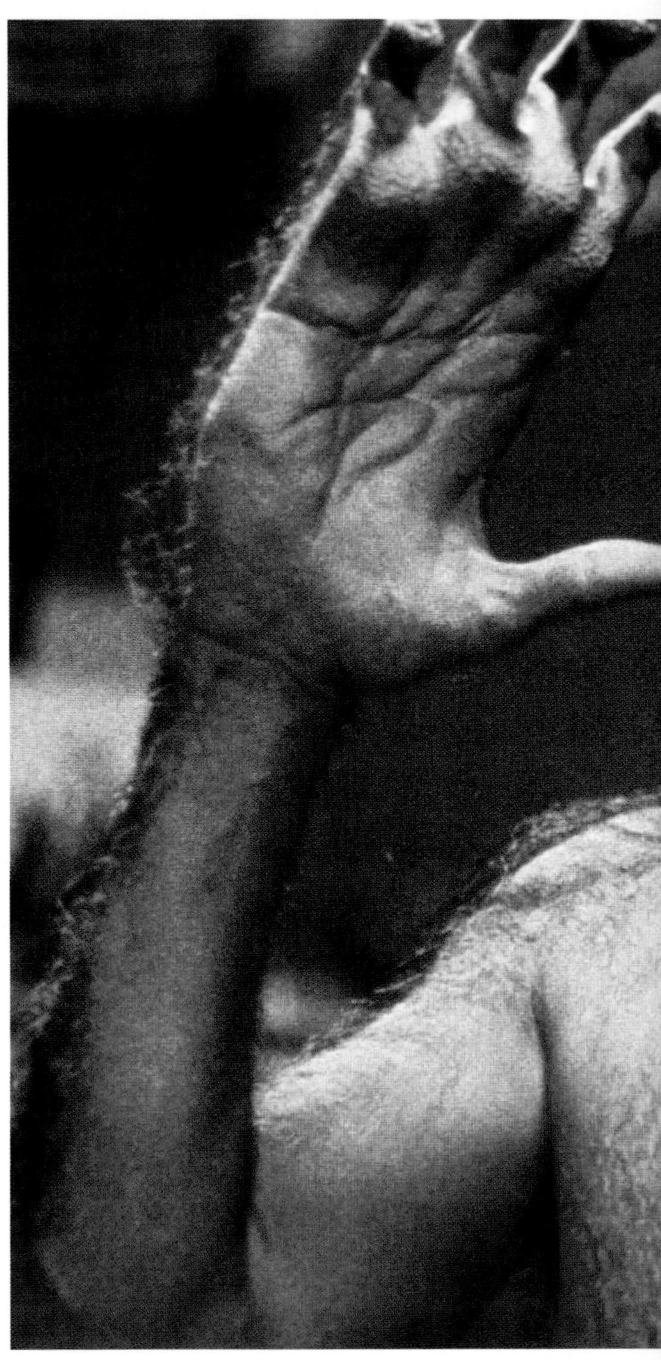

CHANGE HURTS

Changing for the first time comes as a painful surprise to David (David Naughton) in the movie *An American Werewolf in London* (1981). The terrifying transformation takes place in the cozy comfort of his girlfriend's flat, emphasizing the contrast between everyday life and the horrors of the full Moon.

scene and he fights with the wolf man. Using his silver-headed stick he beats it back—and kills it. Maleva arrives and chants her ancient gypsy spell. At this the wolf man transforms back into Larry Talbot. She pronounces his suffering ended, and says he will now find eternal peace. Gwen is unhurt and as her fiancé arrives and holds her tightly, she sinks her face onto his chest, and closes her eyes to what might have been.

THE MEANING OF THE WOLF MAN

There are many important elements in this old, black and white movie. Perhaps the most significant feature is that Larry cannot help but change into the wolf form—even the wise gypsy woman cannot offer him a cure or even a palliative. Nothing can stop him, nothing but the silver weapon he deliberately handed to the man who would release him from this world. Only his self-sacrifice could ensure Gwen would be forever free from his curse. Gwen's love for Larry tempted her away from the straight and narrow path. Like Little Red Riding Hood, she nearly lost her life, but gained a unique insight into Nature's darker mysteries.

Rising again

In fact, the first Wolf Man movie was so popular that the studio (Universal) had Larry Talbot's grave opened one full Moon night, enabling him to rise again and star in *Frankenstein Meets the Wolf Man* (1943). Lon Chaney Jr. was again resurrected as the wolf man in *House of Frankenstein* (1944), and *House of Dracula* (1945), and even made a comedy appearance in *Abbott and Costello Meet Frankenstein* (1948).

AMERICAN WEREWOLF

One of the most popular of all werewolf movies—*An American Werewolf in London* (written and directed by John Landis, 1981)—has a strikingly similar plot to *The Wolf Man*.

Brought up to date, it ticks all the werewolf movie boxes: it has close-up transformation scenes, riveting suspense, laugh-out-loud humor, convincing love, gruesome death, gore by the bucketful and, oh yes, werewolves.

Mystery man

The story begins when two American college students arrive in the desolate North Yorkshire Moor on their European backpacking vacation. As night falls and the full Moon shines, Jack (Griffin Dunne) is attacked and killed by a ravenous creature, and David (David Naughton) is viciously mauled before one of the locals arrives and shoots the beast. As David loses consciousness he sees the slain creature, but it is not the dead animal he was expecting—it's a naked man.

Recovery?

Awaking in a London hospital after being unconscious for almost a month, David finds himself being cared for by an eye-catching young nurse named Alex (Jenny Agutter). One morning he receives an unexpected visitor—Jack. His face is torn and the skin on his neck where he was bitten is flapping around. He is clearly dead.

Jack explains he is in limbo, walking the Earth because his death was unnatural, and the only way out is to end the bloodline of the werewolf that killed: David. Jack urges David to kill himself before he kills others.

Alex, the nurse, invites David to stay with her. He tells her that he's a werewolf, and says he believes a werewolf can only be killed by someone who loves him—just as the werewolf Larry Talbot was killed by his father.

The transformation

Alex works the late shift at the hospital, so David is left on his own at her flat when the full Moon rises. Sitting, reading a book, David suddenly jumps to his feet feeling like he's burning up. He strips off his clothes and is terrified to watch his hands turning into massive paws. Growing hairier by the second, with his leg bones stretching, he cries out for help.

Falling onto all fours, his face begins to change: his teeth grow into fangs, his ears grow points, and the powerful muzzle extrudes in a hideously painful way. Hairy all over, savage and howling, he heads out into the night.

Realization

Several killings later, the morning finds David naked in the wolf enclosure at the zoo. Arriving home he hears about last night's brutal murders, and realizes he must be responsible. He tells Alex he loves her, but that she has to stay away from him as he's not safe to be with. He runs away.

Having phoned his family to say goodbye, David tries to slit his wrists, but he can't kill himself. Jack appears, standing in a cinema doorway. They enter the cinema and find some seats at the back.

The ghosts of the six people David killed appear. Like Jack, they are Earthbound, and they too urge David to kill himself, helpfully suggesting a range of suicide techniques.

Time passes, and once again the full Moon rises. David feels his transformation coming on. Shouting for people to get away, he begins to transform—claws, fangs, killing...

One last gesture

Alex hears about the pandemonium at the cinema and rushes to the scene. She arrives just as the police armed response team are taking positions aiming at the werewolf, who is trapped in a dead-end street. She quickly breaks through the line of police marksmen and approaches the snarling, cornered werewolf.

She tells him they're going to kill him. And, standing beside him, she tells him she loves him. Hearing these words the beast is quietened, for a heartbeat, then leaps toward her. He is hit by a volley of shots from the police.

The curse is broken

David's naked human body lies in the street, riddled with bullets. The curse of the werewolf is broken. He dies instantly, helped by the woman he loved, saving her from himself.

Hope of a Magic Potion

The consequences of transforming into wolf form can be terrible. For werewolves that are forced to transform by a power beyond their control, most famously by the influence of the full Moon, every aspect of their human life is blighted.

We have seen werewolves who would rather die than risk catastrophe by allowing their superhuman urges to be unleashed. Such people may be regarded as heroic in their capacity for self-sacrifice, and noble in the strength of their love for others. Generally, though, they are the exception rather than the rule.

Desperate measures

Offered even the smallest crumb of hope, even the slimmest chance of controlling their transformation and escaping their self-imposed death sentence, most werewolves would gladly accept any risks in order to be free of their dreadful affliction.

In some respects, the 1941 *The Wolf Man* was a remake of an earlier movie—*Werewolf of London* (1935), whose theme was the similarly pessimistic view that the werewolf will seek to kill the one he loves best. Again, this is a love story, and it revolves around the beautiful Lisa (Valerie Hobson) who is torn apart, metaphorically speaking, as events unfold around her. However, in this story the transformation from human to wolf can be prevented by the legendary and almost infinitely rare, phosphorescent wolf-flower, the Mariphasa. This plant carries just a few large flowers that only open in bright moonlight. Each bloom has a thorn at its base.

The werewolf punctures his skin with the thorn and applies the flower to the wound so that its essence enters his bloodstream. It is powerful enough to counteract transformation, but not for any longer than a single night.

Lisa's husband, Dr. Wilfred Glendon (Henry Hull), was collecting a specimen of the Mariphasa in a mysterious valley in Tibet when he was bitten by a werewolf. The creature was described as a Satanic creature, combining the very worst qualities of both man and wolf.

"Transvection"

Wilfred has read that the "transvection" normally occurs between 9 pm and 10 pm on the nights of the full Moon. When he sees fur sprouting on the backs of his hands, and fangs protrude as hair covers his face, he rushes to his laboratory (which is strongly reminiscent of the one in *Dr Jekyll and Mr Hyde*), but the flowers have been stolen by another werewolf named Dr. Yogami (Warner Oland). So Wilfred cannot prevent himself from transforming—or from killing.

When Wilfred discovers Dr. Yogami has not only been stealing his Mariphasa blooms, but was the

werewolf that bit him, passing on the curse, Wilfred flies into a terrible rage and transforms into his wolf form and kills him. Then he breaks into Lisa's bedroom. Lisa flees downstairs, but he jumps down and traps her on the stairs. As he closes in for the kill, she cries out to him, begging him to remember who she is. He is close enough to grab her, but he doesn't—is he remembering the love they shared? Can he gain control over his werewolf nature?

THE WEREWOLF AS MAD SCIENTIST

The werewolf Dr. Wilfred Glendon (Henry Hull) is a botanist with a special interest in the legendary wolf-flower which, according to *Werewolf of London* (1935), can relieve werewolfism. His laboratory could be straight out of the movie of *Dr Jekyll and Mr Hyde*.

A shot rings out. The police have arrived. Wilfred falls and, dying, he thanks the police for the bullet, declaring it was the only way. He says goodbye to Lisa, apologizing that he couldn't make her happier. In death, he transforms back into his human form.

WEREWOLVES IN HARRY POTTER

Even among J.K. Rowling's community of witches and wizards the werewolf is a social outcast, and their company is shunned. The Ministry of Magic sought for centuries to regulate werewolves because all it takes is a single bite to infect any human, magical or not, and then—when the Moon is full—they too will turn into werewolves.

Favorite character

It comes as something of a surprise, then, to discover that professor Remus Lupin is one of J.K. Rowling's favorite characters. He is a friendly yet tragic figure, and is the most significant werewolf in her Harry Potter series of fantasy adventure books and movies. He is both mentally and physically damaged when he is bitten and turned into a werewolf, and he vividly shows young audiences how adults can struggle to find ways of coping with experiences in life.

In his case, there is a herbal potion that can help him control his monthly transformation. Again, it is not a cure, and he needs to ensure he drinks the unpleasant concoction regularly, without fail. His forename commemorates one of the twins of Roman myth—Romulus and Remus (see pages 137–38)—who were suckled as children by a she-wolf, and grew up to found the city of Rome.

A TEACHER WITH A SECRET 

The werewolf Professor Remus Lupin (David Thewlis) has a quiet word with student magician Harry Potter (Daniel Radcliffe) in *Harry Potter and the Prisoner of Azkaban* (2004). Both were attacked by evil early in their lives, and each still suffers the consequences.

In fact, he uses the codename Romulus during the Second Wizarding War. His surname Lupin is a reference to the Latin word *lupus*, meaning wolf. Remus (played in the film by David Thewlis) makes his first appearance in the third instalment: *Harry Potter and the Prison of Azkaban* (book 1999, movie 2004), in which he is introduced to the students at Hogwarts School of Witchcraft and Wizardry as the new Defence Against the Dark Arts tutor.

Hidden depths

His shabby way of dressing and casual attitude disguise his keen intellect and firm commitment to teaching his students. This combination of outer dullness and inner sparkle makes the professor the living embodiment of the saying "you can't judge a book by its cover."

Indeed, his constant efforts to combat his condition, to stop the beast breaking out of him, are a touching and sad reminder that although the curse may be evil, the person suffering can be wholly good.

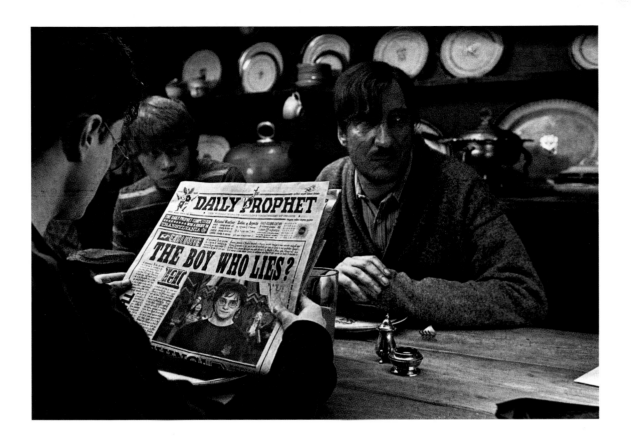

Indoctrination

Remus was a young child when he was bitten by the werewolf Fenrir Greyback, who relishes the taste of human flesh. He targeted children so he could wrest the young werewolves from their parents and indoctrinate them into his mad dream of building a werewolf army to dominate the wizard community. Fenrir's character displays all the hallmarks of the typical tyrant.

Although Remus escaped conscription into Fenrir Greyback's army, he still suffers the agony of transformation every full Moon.

The potion

Headteacher Albus Dumbledore recognizes the goodness in the scholarly Remus, and arranges for him to teach at Hogwarts. There, Remus drinks the recently formulated Wolfsbane Potion, a blue-colored, unpleasant-tasting liquid that smokes slightly. Although it helps control his condition, it is not a cure. It is difficult to make, and is prepared for him by the school's Potions Master, Professor Snape (played by Alan Rickman). When drunk daily in the week approaching the full Moon, Wolfsbane Potion enables a werewolf to turn into a natural wolf during their

transformation, rather than a ravening beast, and to retain their self-control. But even with this help, Remus always misses lessons during the lunar phase of the full Moon, and looks distinctly ill in the days that follow.

Initial moment

Eventually, circumstances prevent Remus from taking the potion. The movie dramatically focuses on the initial moment of transformation, zooming in on the eye as the window to the soul: the bright Moon is reflected in the dark pool of his pupil. The pupil dilates rapidly and the eye becomes bloodshot. Claws burst from the tips of his fingers. His clothes shred and fall off as his back suddenly hunches, and his face contorts as the wolf's long muzzle extrudes.

Fully transformed, he is barely covered by hair, and appears gaunt and thin. Standing on hind legs, he whimpers piteously, but he is still immensely powerful and his instinct is to attack on sight. Later, returned to human form, he decides his secret can no longer be kept, and he resigns from his position at the school.

A useful ally

During the Second Wizarding War against Lord Voldemort, Remus is a member of the Order of the Phoenix (*Harry Potter and the Order of the Phoenix*, book 2003, movie 2007), and despite his introverted personality, he proves to be exceptionally skilled in the wizard's combat of dueling. He also works as a spy and infiltrates the pack of savage werewolves in an attempt to bring them into the fight on Harry's side.

Narrow escape

The tyrannical Fenrir Greyback also fights in the War, but is firmly on the side of the black magician Lord Voldemort. In the Battle of the Lightning-Struck Tower, while Fenrir is in his human phase, he bites and slashes William, "Bill," Weasley, but because he is not in his wolf form, Bill escapes being turned into a werewolf (he does, however, develop a fondness for particularly rare meat).

Close contact

Remus's long involvement with the Order of the Phoenix brings him into close contact with Nymphadora Tonks (played by Natalia Tena), and they fall in love. Remus tries to suppress his feelings because he feels unworthy of her.

None of these excuses makes any difference to the valiant-hearted Nymphadora—or Tonks as she prefers to be known. At the end of *Harry Potter and the Half-Blood Prince* (book 2005, movie scheduled for 2009), Remus is persuaded that his objections are meaningless in the face of love. Remus and Tonks marry at a discreet ceremony in the next book (*Harry Potter and the Deathly Hallows*, 2007).

Groundless worries

He is still tortured, however, by the thought that any children Tonks might bear him could be born as werewolves, which has been known to happen to couples in the past. Fortunately his worries prove groundless, and in the Spring following their marriage he is present at the birth of their son Ted.

The Cure

If controlling monthly outbursts is such a blessing, the prospect of a cure—complete and final—must surely be the Holy Grail of every werewolf. This precious substance is not easily found and, even then, the price may prove to be almost as unbearable as the curse of werewolfism itself.

VAN HELSING

The film *Van Helsing* (2004) shares a certain visual style and gripping intensity with the contemporaneous *Underworld* movies, despite being set in the closing decades of the 19th century. It also shares the same leading lady, in the shape of actress Kate Beckinsale.

If you want a movie that combines werewolves, vampires, and Frankenstein's monster, all rampaging around a splendidly gothic version of Transylvania, then look no further. It even includes references to other werewolf stories, not least of which is a rendition of the famous gypsy verse from *The Wolf Man*.

MIXING MONSTERS

Dracula (Richard Roxburgh) uses werewolves as slaves and unleashes them to hunt and kill his enemies. They are only vulnerable to silver, in the form of bullets or a silver stake through the heart. The werewolf "venom" is transmitted by bite, and the change doesn't take place until the rising of the first full Moon following the attack. Then, the moonlight triggers the physical transformation into a savage bipedal werewolf. The change is not completed, however, until the first stroke of midnight. Before that moment, should the Moon's light be blocked, by a cloud for example, the change stops and the werewolf rapidly reverts into human form. Dracula cannot be killed by ordinary means—only a werewolf can kill him. So, just in case a werewolf is created that he cannot control, he has an antidote ready.

The fatal bite

When monster-fighter Van Helsing (Hugh Jackman) is bitten by a werewolf who is the transformed brother of Anna Valerious (Kate Beckinsale), he needs to find Dracula's cure. As Anna is desperate to kill Dracula, they travel to his castle. Inevitably, parallel interests and the urgent mission bring them close, emotionally as well as physically.

They arrive on the night of the full Moon, and Van Helsing uses his inner wolf's superhuman strength to carry both Anna and a companion Carl (David Wenham) into the castle. Van Helsing confronts the count as the clock chimes the first stroke of midnight, forcing Van Helsing finally to begin his full metamorphosis into his wolf form.

The advantages of being a werewolf

With the physical transformation complete, his strength and agility are more than a match for Dracula. But the vampire exerts an increasingly

Curing the Curse

For one werewolf at least, love is the therapy that cures his condition. In the movie *The Curse of the Werewolf* (1961) a baby boy, Leon, is not only born out of wedlock but on Christmas Day. This combination is an infernal mockery of the Christian nativity and the child is doomed to become a werewolf. He needs close attention because solitude, mistrust, hatred, and vice all strengthen the power of the beast within. Companionship, warmth, virtue, and love empower his human soul to fight with his inner monster. Having grown to manhood, and being frustrated in love, Leon (Oliver Reed) transforms and kills three people at the full Moon—discovering the full magnitude of his curse. When his love Cristina (Catherine Feller) elopes with him, he does not transform. Her love frees him from the evil of the beast. But the authorities are hot on his trail and kill him with a silver bullet. The curse claims him as its final victim.

powerful control over the werewolf, and the fight is in the balance. At the last stroke of midnight, Van Helsing will be completely under the vampire's psychic control. Anna has found the syringe with the antidote to the werewolf venom; she brings it just as he bites and kills Dracula. He sees her, but with bloodlust at fever pitch, he still attacks her.

Moments too late

The chimes of midnight resound through the castle and Van Helsing's companion, Carl, arrives to find the werewolf attacking Anna. He rushes to drive the silver stake into the werewolf's heart, assuming him to be under the complete control of the count. The beast stops him, yet it does not attack. It pulls the syringe from its chest—Anna managed to deliver the antidote.

With his human mind restored already, the werewolf picks up Anna's lifeless body and, as the cure courses through his body, he transforms into his human form. Still holding her in his arms, silhouetted against the full Moon, Van Helsing weeps—his life saved and his heart broken.

THE HEROIC WEREWOLF

Called the "Left Hand of God," Van Helsing (Hugh Jackman) is a monster-hunter on a holy mission in *Van Helsing* (2004). When he becomes a werewolf, he uses his great physical strength in his transformed state to defeat his arch enemy the immortal Dracula.

Living With the Curse

What if you can't find the hidden valley where the Mariphasa grows, or you don't have a Potions Master on hand to help? What if committing suicide is the last thing you want to do? Surely there is some way to help the novice werewolf manage his condition and overcome the dangers of the monthly attack. There is, and it's called learning to cope.

BEING HUMAN

Being Human is an off-beat comedy drama which tells the everyday story of two young men—one a gawky werewolf and the other a handsome but vulnerable vampire—who rent a house in Bristol, UK, only to find there's the ghost of a young woman already "living" there. The series brilliantly envisages life as a werewolf in meticulous and gritty detail. For example, it's a fact that a wolf can digest raw meat much better than a human, so after a successful night's hunting as a wolf, when the transformation back to human is complete, the werewolf is usually physically sick, regurgitating the indigestible remains of his prey. Knowing why something happens is not as good as it not happening, but it's a help.

Coping with adversity

From the beginning, George the werewolf (Russel Tovey) is in denial about his condition and spends

Mitchell Describes George's Change

"He should be dead within 30 seconds. The werewolf's heart is only two-thirds the size of a human's. But to shrink, first it has to stop. In other words, he has a heart attack. All of the internal organs are smaller, so while he's having his heart attack, he's having liver and kidney failure too. If he stops screaming it's not because the pain has dulled, but because his throat, gullet, and vocal chords are tearing and reforming. He literally can't make a sound. By now the pituitary glands should be working overtime, flooding his body with endorphins to ease some of the pain, but that too has shut down. Anyone else would have died of shock long ago. But it won't kill him and that's the thing I find most remarkable. It drags him through the fire and keeps him alive and even conscious to endure every second."

TO BE, OR NOT TO BE...HUMAN

The vampire Mitchell (Aidan Turner, right) tries to convince his friend the werewolf George (Russel Tovey, left) that they can never fit into normal society, in the cult TV series *Being Human* (2009). George ultimately risks his life in a heroic battle to save Mitchell, demonstrating his true humanity.

the whole month desperately trying to forget about his problem, which crops up on the single night of the full Moon. His greatest fear is that he will bite and kill someone. This humanitarian streak is echoed in his friend Mitchell (Aidan Turner), the vampire, who is striving to resist his craving for human blood. The transformation for werewolves, such as George, is particularly painful.

George became a werewolf in 2007 when he was bitten while on holiday in Scotland. Since moving to Bristol he has worked for a year as a hospital porter, and found a disused basement room where he locks himself away during his monthly transformation. When the room is no longer available, he is forced to transform out of doors.

Trying to live normally

Being Human depicts the werewolf as a perfectly normal person with a problem, rather than as a cursed man to be shunned or a savage beast to be shot. George is simply trying to live a normal life. The fact that his entire life is overshadowed by his werewolfism—and the anticipation of the pain he must endure every month—could be seen as an allegory for anyone with a distressing condition.

It's a horrible thing to live with, knowing that at the moment there is no cure, that it is for life. We can't help but admire George deeply, even as we pity him. Even as George learns to live with his problems, he teaches us a new dimension of tolerance and compassion.

Teen Werewolves

THE ALCHEMY OF WRITING

Alchemy is all about transmuting one thing into something else. In most people's minds, an alchemist is somebody who spends their time trying to turn a boring metal, such as lead, into a precious commodity like gold. More often than not, though, he is simply trying to turn a boring life into something worth living.

Authors are alchemists, turning words into ambassadors of wisdom, wit, and wonder. Writers of fiction weave words on the page, which becomes a magic carpet transporting us to where we can walk in their dreams. The curse of the werewolf can be lifted at the stroke of the author's pen. Like a wand, the author's pen can transmute evil into good.

Just imagine

Imagine being free of the monthly compulsion to hunt and kill; imagine being able to control the transformation into a more powerful version of yourself; imagine using your new strength to help people. Imagine being able to do that anytime you like.

TWILIGHT

That is the prospect on offer to the werewolves in Stephenie Meyer's four-book *Twilight* series. Even with its benefits, there is a cost, and it is neither quick nor easy to master the art of controlling the inner beast as it seeks to express itself. But there are elder werewolves who are willing and able to guide the novice as he gets the hang of things.

Although the main plot of the story revolves around a vampire, Edward, and his human lover Bella, their situation is actually a love triangle. Edward has a rival in more senses than one in Jacob, a teenage shape-shifter who turns into a wolf, and who Bella also loves.

Introduced in the first novel, *Twilight* (2005), Jacob is a teenager living on a Native American reservation at La Push, Washington, USA, and a member of the Quileutes tribe. One of their tribal legends indicates they are descended from wolves, and that their ancestors could turn from wolf to man and then back again. It is still taboo to kill wolves in the Quileutes tribe and their only enemy is the vampire.

NEW MOON

In the sequel *New Moon* (2006), Jacob discovers that the tribal legends are true, and he has to come to terms with the fact he is essentially a werewolf. When he transformed for the first time, it was the most terrifying thing that had ever happened to him, but he was comforted and guided by telepathic suggestions from the other members of his pack.

His new responsibilities to the pack involve keeping vampires off their land, and Bella is nearly killed when the pack tracks and slays a vampire who is with her.

Male werewolves

The werewolves are described as being as big as a horse, only more thickset and muscular; their strength and speed is prodigious. They heal abnormally quickly, and remain young so long as they transform fairly frequently. Only the men transform into wolves—with one exception: Leah Clearwater is the only female with the ability.

Jacob, who has formed a strong emotional link with newcomer Bella, is at first tormented by his inability to control the transition, which can often take place unexpectedly.

Like so many werewolves, Jacob fears that he might transform involuntarily when they are together and hurt Bella accidentally. He tries to bring an end to their friendship, as this is the only way he can be sure that she'll be safe. Although he and Bella come to a reconciliation later, Edward cannot agree to the friendship.

ECLIPSE

In *Eclipse* (2007) the shape-shifters reluctantly join forces with Edward and his vampire family, to combat a small army of vampires that arrive to attack Bella and Edward. As he loves Bella, Jacob is particularly concerned about keeping her safe. The invading vampires are destroyed, and although Bella realizes that she loves the stalwart shape-shifter Jacob, she eventually decides that she loves the seductive vampire Edward more.

BREAKING DAWN

The fourth book, *Breaking Dawn* (2008) offers a rare glimpse into the world of the shape-shifter, as the central chapters are written from Jacob's point of view. Of particular note is the pack's reaction to the news that Bella is pregnant with Edward's child. There is concern that the offspring will be abnormal and uncontrollably destructive.

The pack votes to kill both the unborn baby and Bella. Jacob, naturally, disagrees with the decision to kill the woman he loves, and leaves the pack. He is joined by Leah and her brother and forms a new pack, of which he is the alpha male.

Imprinting

Jacob is present at the birth of Bella's baby, who is called Renesmee. The birth is complicated and traumatic for the mother and results in Edward having to save Bella's life by turning her into a vampire (which is what she wanted all along).

Then a remarkable thing happens: Jacob "imprints" on Renesmee, an involuntary act in which a shape-shifter bonds with their soul-mate. He will be devoted to her throughout her life, as a guardian, a brother, a friend, and, if things work out, her lover.

TRADITIONAL WEREWOLF

With the benefits of our enlightened, 21st-century hindsight, we are now able to realize that the traditional image of the werewolf, all scraggy fur and gobbets of blood around the jaws, is a hallowe'en-ish caricature.

A little TLC

Surely the werewolf is actually far more misunderstood than evil, and is a lonely creature in need of help. He needs some tender loving care, and he needs it urgently.

A full day of pampering at a spa would do him a whole world of good. For starters, a thorough shampooing with deep conditioner, followed by slow, relaxing brushing would soon get his pelt shiny and sleek, and his mood more manageable. A pedicure would prevent him from ripping up the carpets every time he takes a step.

A course of anger-management counseling would help give him self-confidence and raise his hunched slouch into a dignified and upright stance. And a little tuition in the basics of dental hygiene would soon floss those shreds of rotting flesh out from between his teeth and cure his bad breath like magic.

And so, with the help of all this pampering, our furry social misfit will begin to feel like a whole new lycanthrope and, instead of turning every social standoff into a bloodbath, he will have poise and self-control enough to join the party and shrug off the raised eyebrows. He will be the ultimate party animal.

TEEN WOLF

Following this image makeover, we arrive at the 1985 hit movie and comedy *Teen Wolf* starring Michael J. Fox as Scott Howard, a 17-year-old high-school student who makes the shocking discovery that he is a werewolf. He is actually a hereditary werewolf, although his father failed to tell him about the "curse" because sometimes it skips a generation, and he didn't want to worry his boy unnecessarily.

A blessing in disguise

Shock turns to delight as Scott learns to control the transformation, becoming a hit on the basketball court with his speed, agility, strength, and charismatic charm as "The Wolf." He also starts winning the attention he craves from the girl of his dreams, and he starts spending most of his time in his wolf form.

Eventually, though, the wonder starts to fade as he realizes the crushing truth that all the new-found success and popularity he has been enjoying really belongs to The Wolf; and The Wolf has a competitive streak that borders on vicious.

BOWLED OVER →

Teenage werewolf Scott (Michael J. Fox) impresses his new lover Pamela (Lorie Griffin) at the bowling alley in *Teen Wolf* (1985). She is one of the many temptations Scott must renounce in order to reclaim his humanity.

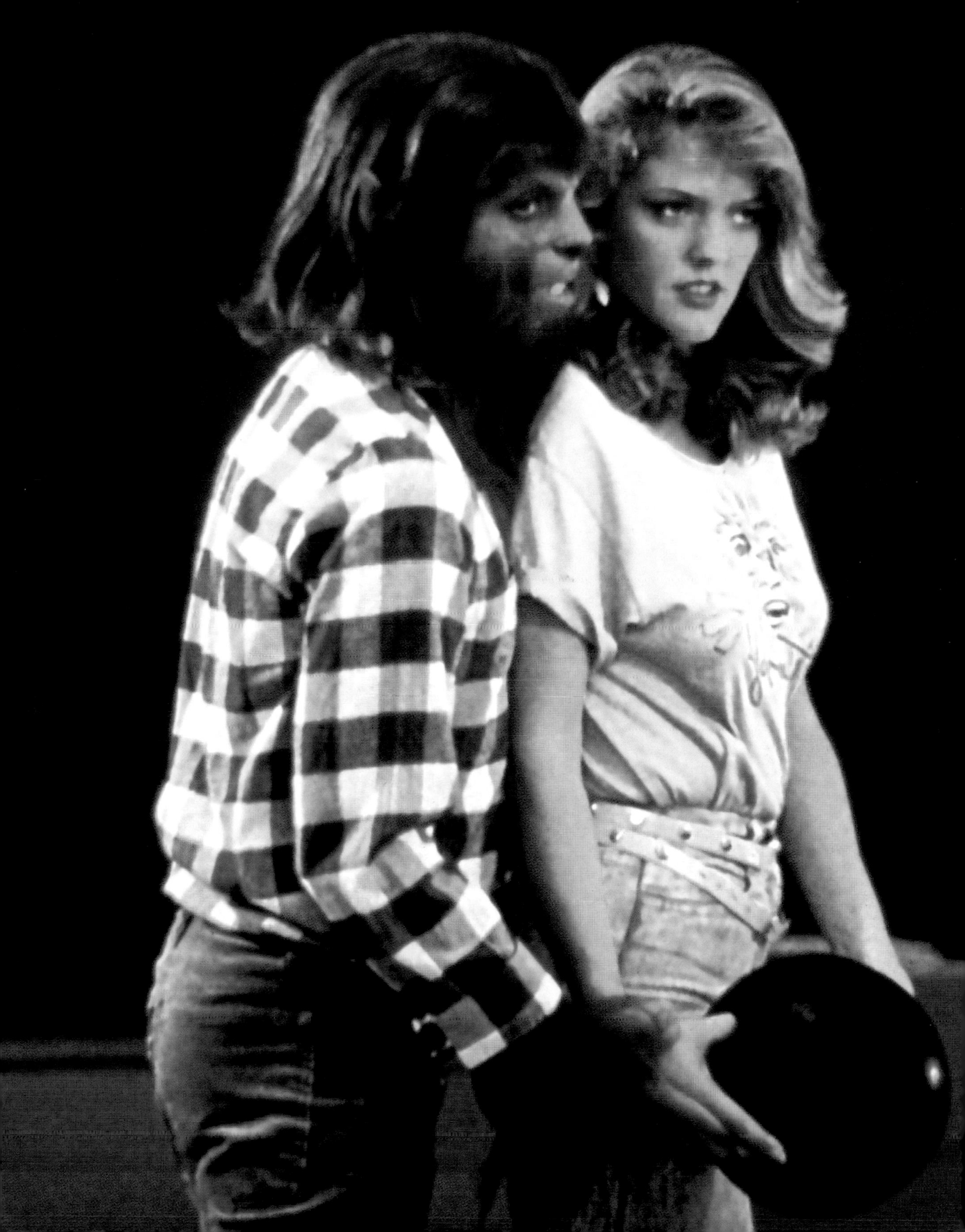

Scott determines to reevaluate his life, and he restrains his increasing addiction to being The Wolf. In this way he shows heroic dedication to his ideals of how life should be lived, which impresses the true love of his life, and inspires the basketball team to achieve victory without relying on his transformation.

THE MUNSTERS

The hit TV comedy series *The Munsters* (Universal Studios, 1963–6) also featured a normal, everyday kid called Eddie, who was a werewolf.

The son of one of Frankenstein's monsters and a beautiful vampire, Eddie tried to live a regular life full of the usual ups and downs of childhood. He is particularly remembered for having a stuffed toy werewolf that looked like Lon Chaney Jr.'s version of the wolf man.

So, from being a terrifying creature of the night, changing to comedy do-gooder and boy-next-door, the werewolf has undergone his biggest transformation yet.

HAPPY FAMILIES

Child werewolf Eddie Munster (Butch Patrick) enjoys a joke with his vampire Grandpa (Al Lewis) on the set of the CBS comedy *The Munsters*, but the famous wolfman doll almost steals the scene. In this episode —My Fair Munster (1964)—Eddie is chased by the local girls after accidentally drinking a love potion.

Movie & TV Werewolves

There are hundreds of movies and TV shows about or including werewolves. Here is a small sample of those not mentioned elsewhere:

- Big Wolf on Campus, *TV series (1999–2000).*
- Discworld Noir, *video game (1999).*
- Dr Terror's House of Horrors, *movie (1965).*
- Dracula, *movie (1992).*
- Europa, *movie (1991).*
- Monster Squad, *TV series (1976–7).*
- She-Wolf of London, *TV series (1990–1).*
- Special Unit 2, *TV series (*The Pack, *Season One, Episode Two, 2001).*
- Supernatural, *TV series (*Heart, *Season Two, Episode 17, 2007).*
- Tales from the Crypt, *TV series (*Werewolf Concerto, *Season Four, Episode 13, 1992).*
- The 10th Kingdom, *TV mini series (2000).*
- The Amazing Screw-On Head, *TV pilot (2006).*
- The Beast Within, *video game (1996).*
- The Chronicles of Narnia; Prince Caspian, *movie (2008).*
- The Hilarious House of Frightenstein, *TV series (1971).*
- Vampire Hunter D, *animated movie (2000).*
- Werewolf, *TV series (1987–8).*
- Wilderness, *TV mini series (1996).*
- Wolf Lake, *TV series (2001–2).*

16th Year of Publication

Weird Tales

25c

AUG.

THE WOLF-GIRL OF JOSSELIN

By ARLTON EADIE

THRILLS!
MYSTERY!
EXCITEMENT!

SEABURY QUINN • • H. THOMPSON RICH • • EDMOND HAMILTON • • GANS T. FIELD

Chapter 3
The She-Wolf

Life of the She-Werewolf

FORMING A PACK

Many she-werewolves live solitary lives, struggling to keep their day-jobs separate from wolfish activities. This makes socializing and dating a real challenge! To remedy this, many make friends among their own, forming a pack.

In the same way as a natural wolf pack, this werewolf pack needs a leader, and she can be female—if she's strong enough. Her strength needs to be more than just physical: she needs wits as sharp as her claws to keep her at the top of the pack. But just as the Moon waxes and wanes, pack leaders come and go, but the pack itself goes on for ever.

THE IMPORTANCE OF THE MOON

The Moon has long been intimately connected with both werewolves and female mysteries. Boldly and invariably changeable, she lights the night with a soft, silver radiance, her crescent may smile down at us, or she may rise red at her fullness, but we know she is always there.

Life originated in the oceans, under the ebb and flow of the tides. We still resonate with them today, if only subconsciously. For the female werewolf, however, that resonance is far stronger. Her life is constrained by the Moon's influence far more powerfully than that of a comparable human: not only will she bleed with the Moon, but she'll transform with her as well.

The monthly curse

The lunar cycle and the cycle of female fertility, known as menstruation, are almost the same length and they are closely linked in people's minds. The very word "menstruation" derives from the Latin *mensis*, meaning "month," and both words have the same Indo-European root as the word Moon. These ideas were all intimately associated in the minds of our ancestors.

The hallmarks of a she-werewolf

What isn't a myth is the common condition premenstrual syndrome (PMS). Symptoms include agitation, irritability, and depression. It is the potential for aggressive reactions and irrational behavior that makes it a serious problem for some women. These are also the hallmarks of a she-werewolf attack, in the sense of losing self-control and venting anger on an innocent bystander.

The theme of menstruation and werewolfism is explored in Peter Beagle's short story *Lila the Werewolf* (1974), a modern tale in which Joe Farrell's new girlfriend brings a few surprises when she moves into his New York home, especially at the coming of the full Moon.

The following two major werewolf movies revolve around the shared theme of the deep and personally disturbing change from child to adulthood in girls, viewed through the magnifying lens of werewolfism.

Silver-Screen Werewolves

THE COMPANY OF WOLVES

As well as being one of the seminal films of the last three decades, *The Company of Wolves* (1984) has been hailed by some as the best werewolf movie yet made, and it succeeds on many levels.

Staggeringly rich in symbolism, and made up of equal parts sensuality and terror, it's a must-see film based on the short story of the same name by Angela Carter. A highly regarded academic feminist and writer of magical realism tales, Carter weaves together the more grizzly side of folk tales into new compositions. The storyline of *The Company of Wolves* is loosely based on the fairytale of Little Red Riding Hood.

Even the special effects for the transformation scenes, which are unsurprisingly crude given their age, are effective because the actors are entirely credible. For their sakes we willingly suspend disbelief, making this nightmarish tour through the dark yet seductive realms of fancy; a beautiful yet subversive delight, directed by the master of the genre, Neil Jordan.

Wish fulfilment

The movie consists of a series of vignettes, presented as the feverish dreams of a modern-day adolescent girl. The first depicts her beautiful yet cruel older sister running through a forest, being chased and eventually caught by a pack of Alsatian dogs. It is a simple "wish-fulfilment" dream in which the impersonal appetite of the beasts is unleashed to devour her enemy.

The same vast, wild wood sets the gloomy, yet occasionally enchanting, scene for all the tales that follow. The stories focus on Rosaleen (Sarah Patterson), an innocent peasant girl who is gradually awakening to the monstrous power and sublime seduction of physical love.

Rosaleen is captivatingly beautiful and is courted by the blacksmith's son, but although she genuinely likes the lad, she does not fall for his advances. She is enthralled by the cautionary tales her Granny tells, which talk of wolves that are hairy on the outside, and warn of men who are hairy on the inside—werewolves.

Shock ending

The ending of this movie comes as a surprise, and has left many viewers feeling vaguely bewildered. However, in context, it makes symbolic sense: the adolescent girl in whose feverish dreams all these stories have been played out, awakes to the pack of animals flowing through the dusty, dying house of her old, childish life, smashing all the toys and trivial keepsakes once so dear to the heart of the child she was such a short time ago. The reality of the situation sinks in—they have come for her, carrying with them all the dangers and desires of her adult life.

If we study the story closely we find clues to its deeper meanings. For instance, the Moon is full on the night of Rosaleen's final ordeal, and it turns a smoldering red. But this is more than a signal of danger—even the vivid color of the girl's hooded cloak is associated with menstruation. Our heroine is no longer a child, but her initiation into womanhood is bloody in more ways than one.

Modern she-wolves

A large part of the process of adolescence, with its seemingly haphazard rebelliousness, is focused on the search for independence. And the price we pay for that freedom is the loss of innocence. We cease to trust blindly and follow advice; our parents are no longer the gods keeping us safe in our personal garden of Eden.

A world of our own

But we are not cast out of that paradise; we leave of our own accord, and although return to that innocent state may be impossible, we are free to find a world of our own when we follow the wolf.

TRANSFORMATION FROM CHILD TO WOMAN

Rosaleen (Sarah Patterson) takes the fateful step and willingly enters the realm of the werewolves in Neil Jordan's masterpiece *The Company of Wolves* (1984), a movie version of Angela Carter's retelling of the Little Red Riding Hood story.

GINGER SNAPS

Another classic movie that overlays the emotional and physical changes of female puberty, with the metamorphosis of werewolfism, is the Canadian movie *Ginger Snaps* (2000).

Suburban quasi-goth Ginger Fitzgerald (Katharine Isabelle) is obsessed with death and is planning her own suicide. She has formed a blood pact to take her younger sister Brigitte (Emily Perkins) with her, but then everything changes when Ginger has her first period, which coincides with the full Moon.

Fatal attraction

They go out that night to play a prank on a girl who has badly upset Brigitte. As the younger sister, Brigitte is sensitive, retiring, and easily led by her older sister.

While they are out, a werewolf is attracted to Ginger by the scent of her menstrual blood, and viciously attacks her in the woods beside the local playground. Brigitte manages to beat the werewolf away, and it is run over and killed by a passing van.

In denial

Back at home, Brigitte pleads for Ginger to go to hospital. But Ginger is in denial about the strange events that have taken place, and the deep bite marks on her shoulder heal supernaturally quickly. Ginger is also now growing increasingly irritable. Within a few days, her scars have started to sprout fur and she has started to grow a thin, naked tail.

A silver ring

Brigitte finds an ally in Sam, who knows something about werewolves. He suggests wearing a pure silver ring in a piercing, hoping that the folklore about the precious metal might counteract the werewolf infection, but it has no effect at all on her gradually strengthening transformation.

Wolfsbane potion

The next full Moon coincides with Hallowe'en, and Brigitte locks Ginger in the bathroom. Brigitte gets Sam to concoct a potion of monkshood to help her sister; he advises the safest way to administer it is by injection.

Before she can get home with the potential antidote, she encounters Jason—who has been infected with the werewolf curse by Ginger. He is attacking a young boy, and when Brigitte stops him, he attacks her. She uses her precious syringe on him, and it works rapidly.

Arriving at the happy ending that is promised by this breakthrough is not, unfortunately, straightforward. As Ginger loses her battle of control over her wolfish state, she becomes increasingly violent and unpredictable.

Transformation

Ginger's journey of transformation is particularly memorable for the effect it has on her younger sister, Brigitte. For its themes of adolescent love, suicide, drugs, sex, sibling rivalry, feminism, humor, horror, and last but not least, werewolves, *Ginger Snaps* has a strong cult status.

Female Characters

A selection of other books of werewolf fiction with strong female characters.

- Bad Blood, *L.A. Banks (2008). Sequel:* Bite the Bullet *(2008);* Undead on Arrival *(2009).*
- Bitten, *Kelley Armstrong (2001). Sequels:* Stolen *(2002);* Broken *(2006).*
- Heart of the Wolf, *Terry Spear (2008). Sequels:* Don't Cry Wolf *(2009);* To Tempt a Wolf *(2009).*
- Moon Called, *Patricia Briggs (2006). Sequels:* Blood Bound *(2007);* Iron Kissed *(2009);* Cry Wolf *(2008).*
- The Sight, *David Clement-Davies (2002). Sequel:* Fell *(2007).*
- Through Wolf's Eyes, *Jane Lindskold (2001). Sequels:* Wolf's Head, Wolf's Heart *(2002);* The Dragon of Despair *(2003);* Wolf Captured *(2004);* Wolf Hunting *(2006);* Wolf's Blood *(2007).*
- Wilderness, *Dennis Danvers (1991).*

FACING AN UNCERTAIN FUTURE 

The bonds of sisterly love are tested to breaking point when Ginger (Katharine Isabelle, left) is bitten and begins to transform into a werewolf. Brigitte (Emily Perkins, right) faces a terrifying dilemma in *Ginger Snaps* (2000).

The Lone She-Werewolf

There is a tradition of lone, female werewolves being lured by the comforts of home life to try to settle down and raise a family with a mortal man, but their inner wildness usually brings the relationship to a premature end.

THE SHE-WOLF

A remarkable story of a free spirit that comes to dwell for a while in the coziness of human habitation is told in the traditional Croatian folk tale entitled simply *The She-Wolf*. It was collected by A.H. Wratislaw in his *Sixty Folk-Tales from Exclusively Slavonic Sources* (1890).

An old mill lies abandoned because everyone believes it is enchanted, haunted by a she-wolf. One day a soldier takes shelter there, makes a fire in the grate, goes upstairs, bores a small hole in the wooden floor to look through, and waits to see what happens.

"Skin down"

That night, a she-wolf comes in. She says "Skin down, skin down, skin down" and stands up on her hind legs, shakes herself, and her wolf's skin slips off and falls to the ground. Out of the skin steps a beautiful young woman.

She hangs the wolf-skin on a peg, goes to the fire, and settles down to sleep. The soldier creeps downstairs, steals her wolf-skin and hides it. Then he returns to the maiden and wakes her in the morning. She starts to scream, "Skin on me. Skin on me. Skin on me." But her skin doesn't come to her call. After some time has gone by, the couple marry and have two children. One day the eldest boy tells his mother he has heard that she is a wolf. She denies it, calling it nonsense: "If I am a wolf, where is my skin?" The child goes to ask his father about it all, and his father says it is true. The boy asks, "Where is her skin?" And the man shows him. When the boy sees his mother again, he cries, "Mama, you are a wolf—your skin is on the mill wheel." With a kiss, she says, "Thank you, my child, for rescuing me." She leaves, and is never seen again.

SKIN-DEEP

Similar to the legend of the Scottish *selkie*, the seal women who are also forced to remain in human form if anyone hides their seal-skin, the story warns the reader about the dangers of treachery. It also reminds us that our humanity is really only skin-deep—underneath lurks the wolf.

A curious tale from medieval Ireland turns this premise on its head: instead of a she-wolf masquerading as a woman, the woman temporarily becomes a she-wolf. Again, the wolf's pelt is removed to reveal the woman within.

RELIGIOUS WEREWOLVES

Saint Natalis, who lived in the 6th century, is said to have laid a curse on the descendants of those

who live in Ossory, Leinster, Ireland: every seven years a couple has to abandon their home and take to the woods to live as wolves. The tale is told by Gerald of Wales (c.1146–c.1223) in the *Topographia Hibernica,* Section Two, Chapter 19.

In 1182 or 1183, a priest and his traveling companion are passing through the woods near Ossory, and have made camp for the night, when a wolf approaches their fire. The travelers are astonished when the wolf speaks, telling them not to be afraid.

Current victims

The werewolf describes what the saint has done and explains that he and his wife are the current victims of the curse. They have already been wolves for two-thirds of their allotted span, and would, if they survive the remainder, return to their human lives in due course. However, he adds, his wife is seriously ill and in urgent need of the priest's services.

The three of them go to a large, hollow tree and find the she-wolf there. She groans and sighs as if she is close to death. The priest hears her confession and forgives her sins, but he will not complete the last rites, as he feels unable to give the Eucharist to an animal.

The werewolf gently places his claw on his wife's head, and draws down her fur, revealing the human head of an old woman. When the pelt has been drawn down all the way to her waist the priest sees she is indeed human, and he relents and administers the sacrament. Then the werewolf lifts up her wolf skin, covering her fully once more. We are not told of the she-wolf's fate, merely that the priest and his companion leave the forest safely. The fact that religion is involved reinforces the fact that they are still people.

THE PHANTOM SHIP

The theme of the solitary female werewolf who takes on a woman's role is also explored in the novel *The Phantom Ship* (1839) by Frederick Marryat, who was one of the first authors to introduce the character of the she-wolf.

Though part of a larger work, the episode with the she-wolf has been reprinted on its own as a short story *(The White Wolf of the Hartz Mountains),* and is essentially a tale of passion, revenge, and retribution. It inspired numerous authors to use similar motifs in their own tales, notably Sir Gilbert Campbell in his *The White Wolf of Kostopchin* (1889). Since then, many authors have indulged in the romance and glamor of dressing their beautiful female werewolves in coats of soft, white, decadent fur.

Having killed his wife and her lover in a crime of passion, misogynistic character Krantz is forced to flee from his home in Transylvania. He and his

three young children settle in central Germany in an isolated cottage in the densely forested Hartz Mountains. Here, Krantz ekes out a living by hunting and growing such food as he can.

A white wolf

One day, in the depths of Winter, he sees a white wolf whose pelt would be particularly valuable, so he stalks it deep into the snowy wilderness. It almost seems to be leading him on, for each time he gets within range of his rifle the she-wolf bounds away, only to let him catch up a little higher on the mountain. Then, in one of those haunted spots all huntsmen know and avoid, the precious prize stands and waits while Krantz takes careful aim.

In that strange open space in the pine forest, she vanishes. Krantz is confused and miserable at losing his quarry, but then he hears the hushed note of a distant huntsman's horn. It is a distress call and he answers its plea. He finds two exhausted travelers: Wilfred and his daughter, Christina. Krantz offers them hospitality, which they gratefully accept.

The children take an instant dislike to the beautiful young woman with the sparkling eyes, overly large mouth, and shining teeth. But Krantz falls completely under her spell. When he asks her father for permission to marry her, Wilfred agrees to perform the ceremony himself.

A solemn oath

Wilfred adds one condition, however, that Krantz swears by the Spirits of the Mountains never to harm Christina, with the sinister penalty that if he breaks his word, both he and his children will die horribly and the Spirits—in the form of wild beasts—will take revenge.

A dramatic change

As soon as they are married, Christina changes completely, treating the children with great cruelty. They also see she has some odd habits, leaving the house for an hour every night, during which time they hear a wolf outside. The children investigate. To protect her secret, Christina kills two of them.

When she is seen eating one of them, Krantz shoots her. But it is not the body of Christina he finds slumped over the child's remains, but a large, white she-wolf. It is the same wolf that had lured him to find Christina those few short months ago, and now Krantz understands he has been deceived by the Spirits of the Mountains—who have power over murderers.

WEREWOLVES IN BUFFY

The story reminds us that one consequence of giving in to a murderous passion is that one enters a world in which the murderer is liable to become the victim. This moral theme is echoed in *Wild at Heart* (1999, Episode Two, Season Four of *Buffy the Vampire Slayer*).

Here, a beautiful young singer has embraced her werewolfism, with all its strength and savagery, and regards her human form as a mere disguise that has to be maintained until the full Moon returns to set her free for a while.

Veruca (Paige Moss) can only transform during the three nights closest to the full Moon, and invariably wakes up naked in the morning as her clothes are destroyed during the transformation. Unlike younger werewolves, she can remember exactly what has happened in her wolf phase.

Instant attraction

When she meets Oz (Seth Green), who is also a werewolf, they feel an immediate attraction even though they are both in human form. Oz usually spends the full-Moon nights in a cage to make sure he doesn't hurt anyone, but this time he breaks free and finds Veruca. In the morning they wake up together. That night he persuades her to spend the night with him in his cage, which she accepts. Oz's girlfriend Willow (Alyson Hannigan) finds them together and is distraught.

That evening, Veruca in her wolf form corners Willow, but Oz arrives just in time to stop Veruca killing her. In the fight Veruca is killed, but Willow is still not safe as Oz is out of control. Her best friend Buffy (Sarah Michelle Gellar) arrives and tranquilizes him. Oz decides that he is simply too unsafe to be near Willow, and leaves to learn some meditation techniques in Tibet. These will free him from the regular monthly transformations, although intense emotions could still trigger the change.

TRUE TALES

Summary justice, a lynching really, was handed out in northern Hungary, in or around 1881, and the story is told in the *Journal of the Gypsy Lore Society* (1892).

Kropan, a Romany fiddler, works late each night playing music in the local inns, but what he receives in wages is barely enough to keep him and his wife alive. One night he notices his wife is no longer hungry. He suspects she is having an affair with a more affluent man and starts to spy on her. Coming home unexpectedly early he is startled to see a great wolf loping out of their house. He searches for his wife, but cannot find her, and is grief-stricken in the belief that the beast has devoured her. With nowhere else to go, he lies down on their bed, but cannot sleep.

The wolf returns

In the twilight of morning he sees the wolf return, carrying a sheep in its jaws. Astonished, he watches it drop the sheep, turn around in a circle, and instantly transform into his wife. She calls to him that they have food enough and that she will cook them a roast dinner. From that time forward, every night she becomes a wolf and goes hunting, returning with more meat than they can eat. Indeed, Kropan begins to sell the extra, and eventually opens his own inn.

Eventually the werewolf's supply of livestock from the surrounding villages becomes exhausted, but instead of being content with what she has already supplied, she starts marauding in her own neighborhood.

One night she kills the priest's own pet lamb, and he recognizes the carcass when he sees it in their inn. The priest senses the presence of evil and casts holy water about the building, onto Kropan, and onto his wife—she screams as if drenched in boiling oil, and disappears. Kropan, however, is seized and killed by the outraged villagers. Official justice condemns two of the mob's ringleaders to six years in prison for the murder of the Romany fiddler, who had settled and thrived in the heart of their community. But the werewolf wife who brought food in desperate times, and who has grown too greedy, or perhaps loved to hunt and kill too much, is never heard of again.

FRENCH FOLK TALE

Another dreadful tale of an apparently good wife who is accused of being a werewolf, is set in 1558 near the village of Apchon in the region of Auvergne, France. It is supposed to be true.

Trophy

One evening a trusted huntsman meets the local landowner who is passing by. The landowner asks him to bring something from the night's hunt back to his chateau. The huntsman promises he will and goes on his way. In a deserted valley he is attacked by a particularly large wolf. He fires his gun but misses the beast. With his hunting knife swiftly drawn, he slashes at the wolf, severing its paw. Howling, the wolf escapes, leaving the huntsman unhurt.

Recognition

He puts the trophy in his pouch and, knowing the chateau is near by, visits the wealthy landowner to tell his tale. He reaches into his pouch for the grisly item to show, but what he brings out is no shaggy paw of a wolf, but the delicate hand of a woman of leisure—and it wears a gold ring the man recognizes instantly. He rushes to his wife's suite to find her in some distress, with one forearm swathed in bandages. At his insistence she reveals the wound—her hand is missing. She subsequently confesses that she is the wolf that attacked the huntsman. She is condemned to death and burnt.

THE WEREWOLF

A different take on the lone she-werewolf was adopted by the earliest-known werewolf movie. *The Werewolf* was a short film made in 1913, but the only known copy was destroyed in a fire in 1924. It was based on a short story by Henry Beaugrand (*The Wer-Wolves*, 1898) and told the story of a Navajo woman, Kee-On-Ee.

When her white husband disappears, Kee-On-Ee believes she has been betrayed and abandoned by him, whereas in fact he has been killed. She nurtures her mistrust of men into hatred and she becomes a witch.

Kee-On-Ee raises her daughter, Watuma, in the same dark craft, and with the same extreme loathing of white men. With the power of a Skinwalker, Watuma turns into a werewolf at will, and metes out her vengeance to all who fall into her grasp, but she is eventually stopped by a Christian friar. However, her mother returns from the grave one hundred years after her death, to exact revenge on the reincarnation of the man who had killed her husband, by killing his lover.

Love and death, the twin themes of so many werewolf stories, echo the two opposing sides of the werewolf's own accursed nature.

Running With the Pack

THE IMPORTANCE OF THE PACK

We have seen some of the difficulties that beset the lone she-wolf, the worst of which is when she needs help and there is nobody around who can understand and support her. Therefore, being a member of a pack with an all-for-one and one-for-all attitude of extreme loyalty for each other, can have tremendous appeal.

Responsibilities

Clearly, having the backup of an entire pack can be invaluable and even save your life. But with the benefits come responsibilities to the other pack members, especially to the pack leaders—the alpha male and alpha female. Sometimes it isn't easy to fit in with what everybody else wants to do.

KITTY AND THE MIDNIGHT HOUR

How it feels to be the youngest and newest member of a werewolf pack is explored in the sassy, witty, and insightful book *Kitty and the Midnight Hour* (2005).

This is one of the most readable werewolf novels to have been published in recent years, and it is the first of six books in the *Kitty* series. Bestselling and prolific author Carrie Vaughn has created a truly remarkable modern werewolf heroine.

Kitty Norville is young, free, and single, and a closet werewolf. Each full Moon she runs with the pack through the wilds of Denver, USA, but the rest of the time she's just an ordinary citizen trying to make ends meet.

Being a cub

She is the latest addition to the werewolf pack, and is treated like a cub. She behaves that way too, painfully aware of her mistakes and constantly trying to appease the more dominant members of the pack. With Carl, the alpha male, whose charisma makes everyone in the pack love and obey him unquestioningly, she is completely submissive, scared, and dying to please him in every way.

Keeping a grip on reality

Her local pack is drawn from an area with a radius of a couple of hundred miles (around 300 km), and only meets at full Moon when all werewolves must change.

But other packs enjoy the freedom of their wolf form so much that they spend as much time as possible as wolves. The wolf state can be addictive, and Kitty is desperate to keep her humanity intact and not give in to the lure of the wolf within her.

Werewolves on the airwaves

Kitty has a late-night slot on a local radio station playing music and taking calls from the public. When a caller starts discussing conspiracy

theories about vampires, Kitty is tempted to reach out to people, like herself, who are still coming to terms with encounters with the secret side of life.

Phone-in

She invites listeners to phone in and talk to her live on air to share their experiences with vampires and, yes, werewolves. The ratings start to soar, and her weekly show—*The Midnight Hour*—is taken up by other radio stations: Kitty is syndicated.

But Carl, the alpha male, is unhappy and believes her show threatens the secrecy, and therefore the security, of the werewolf pack. Kitty is torn between her loyalty and devotion to Carl and her pride in and love for her radio show. For the first time in her life, she feels more angry than scared, and she carries on with the show and talks him around into accepting it.

Exile and change

Eventually, though, Kitty is exiled from the pack and must leave her job and friends in Denver,

AN IMPOSSIBLE LOVE →

A tale of passion and betrayal is woven between the worlds of humans and werewolves. The story of *Blood and Chocolate* was converted into a movie in 2007 (which is notably different to the book). In this shot heroine Vivian (Agnes Bruckner) is shown with her love Aiden (Hugh Dancy).

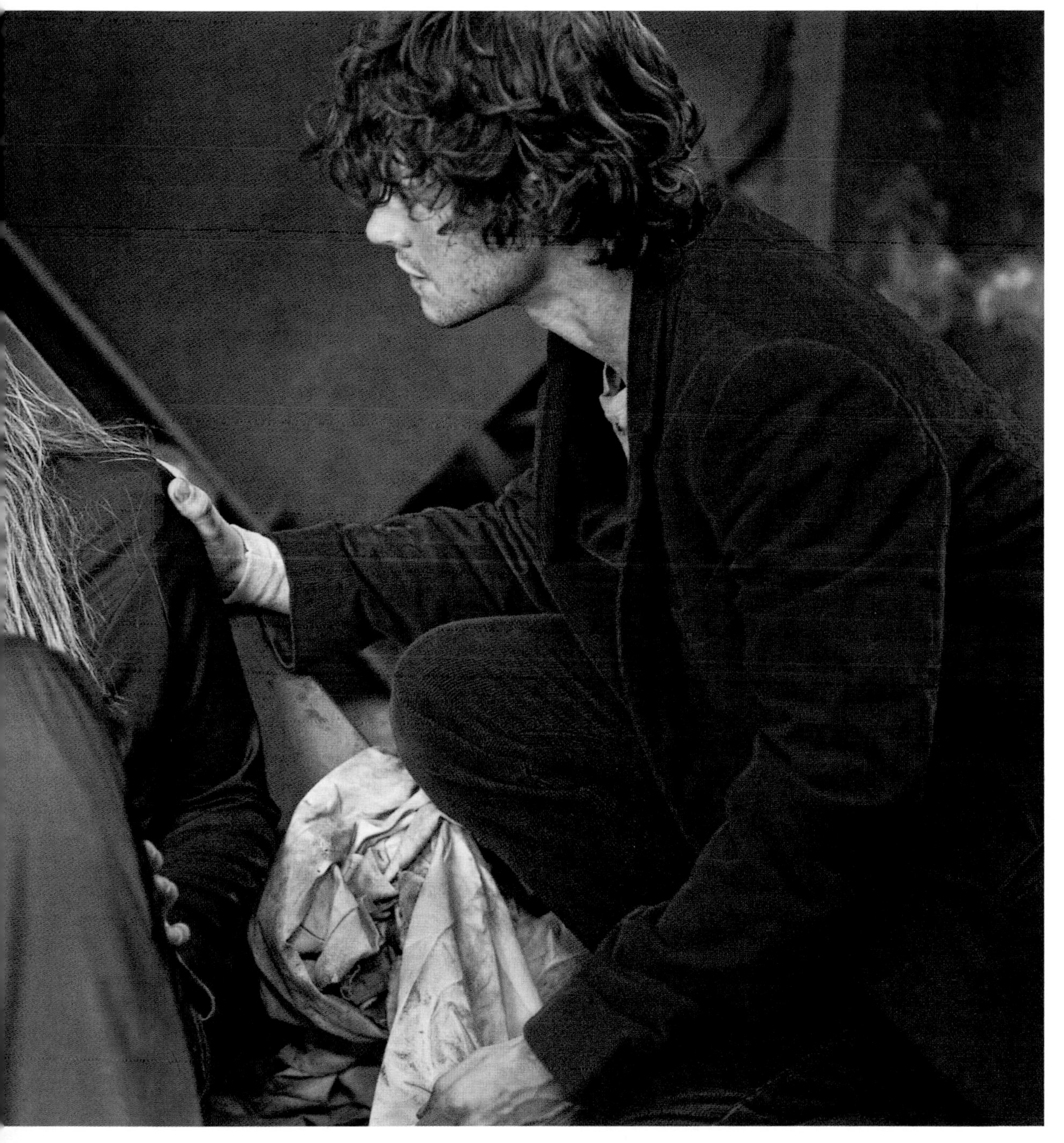

too. She must learn to survive on her own. Although changing from human to wolf is painful it is fairly straightforward. Reverting to human form, however, involves losing consciousness, which makes her very vulnerable.

Animal kingdom

The book's descriptions of the pack hierarchy and its customs are vivid and visceral, sparing the reader nothing—including the fact that the alphas get to mate, and with anyone they want.

Kitty's struggles to retain her humanity, while still relishing her wolf-life, are poignant, as are her ways of coping with the strain of the physical transformation. By concentrating on the mental image of flowing water, she is able to keep herself from feeling her joints and muscles warping into new configurations and her bones sliding beneath her skin.

Making her own life

But mostly it is Kitty herself—her determination to make her own life despite what the alpha male has to say about it—that stands out. She is forced to choose between safety and her own desires, and she chooses to become a lone wolf with the distant prospect of forming a pack of her own if she can survive that long.

BLOOD AND CHOCOLATE

The opposite situation is detailed in the novel *Blood and Chocolate* (1997), which also explores the consequences of having one's life controlled by the pack. The question is—if we were faced with the choice, which path would we take?

It's certainly not easy being a teenage girl in a werewolf pack whose members are literally at each other's throats as they compete to be its new leader. Add the spicy ingredient of forbidden love, and you have a recipe for the sort of success enjoyed by this romantic mystery novel by Annette Curtis Klause (which was released as a rewritten movie with the same name in 2007.)

The power of the Moon

Vivian is sixteen years old, beautiful but reserved, and she is also a werewolf. She is a member of the *loups-garoux* (French for werewolves), who became a separate species—*Homo lupus*—when their ancestors were blessed by the Moon goddess, Selene, with the ability to shape-shift.

Although they can transform at will, the power of the Moon is impossible for them to resist, and they must transform every full Moon.

Moving with the pack

Vivian's pack was attacked and hounded from their old home in West Virginia, an event in which her father died, and has just moved to a sleepy suburb in Maryland, USA. Vivian's father had been the alpha male of the werewolf pack, and now rivalry and confusion are running riot, threatening to tear the pack apart.

At her new high school, Vivian falls in love with shy, sensitive Aiden, but she is in an agony of indecision over whether or not she can trust him with her great secret. She is torn between her human self, which is sweet as chocolate, and her wild wolf form, whose nature is as dark as blood.

The "Old Way"

To find the new alpha male for her *loups-garoux* pack, the candidates invoke the "Old Way" and fight for dominance in an ancient ceremony called the "Ordeal." The physical combat is decided by bloodshed—whoever bleeds loses. Gabriel, who is 24 years old, wins.

The Bitches' Dance

The fight to find Gabriel's mate, the new alpha female, is decided in the parallel ritual of the "Bitches' Dance." While Vivian has no interest in the contest, she steps in to prevent her mother being killed. Vivian saves her mother and wins the bout, which means she is automatically selected as the new alpha female. By right, she is destined to be Gabriel's consort.

But Vivian is still in love with Aiden, and runs to him, revealing her true self. He is horrified and she runs away. Aiden has a silver pentagram pendant made into a bullet and ambushes her, but before he can shoot her, Gabriel arrives.

Stuck

Aiden aims and fires at Gabriel, but Vivian instinctively protects him and takes the bullet herself. Gabriel removes the bullet before it kills her (silver is a poison to *loups-garoux* blood), but she is badly hurt and her body is stuck in mid-transformation between her human and wolf forms—the worst of both worlds.

Gabriel is genuinely attracted to her and confesses that he too once loved a human, but had accidentally killed her. Vivien accepts that perhaps, after all, the two species should stay separate. With her renewed commitment to her pack and a kiss of love with her new partner, Gabriel, she finds her body is healed and she is free to transform again.

The distinction

The story explores several elements central to werewolves: primarily, it brings into sharp contrast the distinction between werewolves and humans and raises questions of how right or ethical it is even to try to unite the two worlds. It also shows how bitterly divisive and distressing it can feel to be an outsider, excluded from a world one desperately wishes to join.

In Vivien's case, native good sense wins out, and her ending is a more or less happy one, though not what she had originally wanted. Sometimes, she might say, "we have to give up our dreams in order to reach our goals."

THE WOLF-GIRL

Romance flowering in a quiet country town is a theme that features strongly in the story of *The Wolf-Girl of Josselin* by Arlton Eadie, published in the magazine *Weird Tales* (August 1938).

The medieval town of Josselin, Brittany, France, was not always as welcoming to strangers as it is today. Its ancient legend tells us that one day, while the women of the town were drawing water and washing clothes at the fountain, a young woman with a small baby came up to them and begged for alms. The women spurned her and set their dogs on her.

A curse

It is at this point that the author departs from the legend. He says that the young woman's baby has died, and just before she also died she cursed the women of Josselin to transform periodically into a pack of wolves. That night they do indeed, and each mother slays her male children.

The triumph of maternal love

The curse continues for centuries, affecting only mothers. Then, a young Englishman visits and falls in love with a young Josselin girl. They marry, but when their son is born, the curse claims her as its newest victim, and she nearly murders the boy. But maternal love triumphs in the end.

Virgin Mary

The legend told in the town today differs in that the beggar was none other than an apparition of the Virgin Mary, and instead of turning the women into a pack of wolves, she merely made them, or some of their children, bark like dogs.

THE PARDON

Throughout Brittany, France, there is a strong tradition of the "pardon," a popular religious festival where pilgrims come to receive the mercy of divine revelation, intervention, and the cure of physical ailments.

The festival of the Pardon of Josselin is held every year on 7th and 8th of September, at the Church of Notre Dame de Ronciers (Our Lady of the Brambles.) This is believed to be named after a miraculous statue of the Virgin Mary was found in a bramble patch.

Cures

The festival used to be called the *Pardon des Aboyeuses* (pardon of the barkers) and was particularly devoted to curing ailments whose symptoms involved barking, and miraculous cures have been claimed. It's an interesting inversion of the usual religious abhorrence and intolerance shown toward all otherworldly creatures, who are usually deemed to be evil, cursed, or possessed by devils. It may even imply a certain sympathy for those cursed to be werewolves.

Brittany has a long association with werewolves, and superstitions were rife, including the idea that the illegitimate son of a priest would be doomed to become a *den-bleiz* (man-wolf) or *bleizgarv* (wolf-rude), both terms equivalent to "werewolf."

The Isle of Sein, off the extreme west coast of Brittany, was reputed by the Roman geographer, Pomponius Mela, (writing around 43 CE) to be home to a coven of women who were able to transform into the shape of any animal.

STRANGER THAN FICTION

The timid wolf-girl Danielle Dax (*The Company of Wolves*, 1984) retreats from the human world into the shelter of "the world below." She was shot and wounded on her first venture above ground. Although her wounds heal, she will never again dare to meet the creatures that greeted her with fear and bullets.

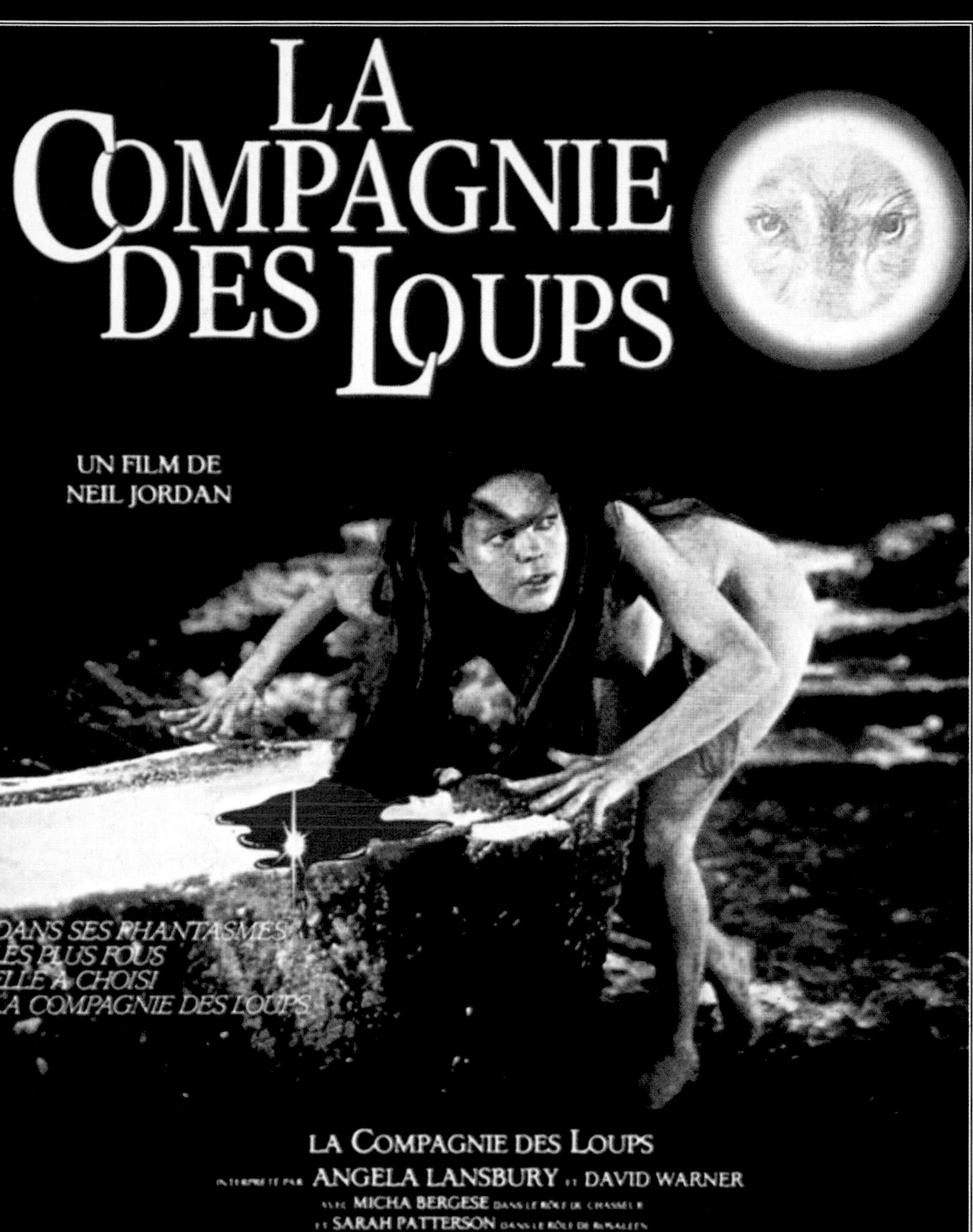
LA COMPAGNIE DES LOUPS
UN FILM DE NEIL JORDAN
DANS SES PHANTASMES LES PLUS FOUS ELLE À CHOISI LA COMPAGNIE DES LOUPS
LA COMPAGNIE DES LOUPS
ANGELA LANSBURY ET DAVID WARNER
MICHA BERGESE
SARAH PATTERSON
CHRISTOPHER TUCKER
GEORGE FENTON
ANGELA CARTER ET NEIL JORDAN
STEPHEN WOOLLEY ET NIK POWELL
CHRIS BROWN ET STEPHEN WOOLLEY

The Alpha Female

In the pack, status is worth more than gold—it can determine who lives and who dies. Competition for status is intense, and fighting between pack members is as commonplace as it is bloody. This rivalry keeps the pack in peak physical condition and ensures that all the members have well-honed battle skills.

STRONG BONDS

Although fitness is a key survival tool, a pack's real strength comes from the bond of friendship and mutual trust between its members. This relationship keeps the pack close-knit, and prevents it from destroying itself. In times of crisis, this fierce devotion to protect every member, regardless of personal feelings, and to rely on them supporting you, is the key to success.

The greatest challenge of the alpha female is in maintaining the balance between the ever-smoldering (and often explosive) tension among individuals and the rock-solid cohesion of the pack as a whole. If she fails in this, she will be summarily dismissed and instantly replaced. But if she is successful, her reward is the certain knowledge that her every whim and desire will enjoy the guaranteed backing of the whole pack.

Full power

Wherever she goes she has the full power of the pack behind her—male and female—all its muscle, all its cunning and resolve; hers to command through unquestioning loyalty. With many pairs of eyes vigilantly on the lookout all around for threats, and even more teeth willing and able to protect her from every side, she is as close to being invincible as any she-wolf can be. But it is lonely at the top.

The object of attention

There will always be males in the pack who would risk a raking from her claws to become her mate. Sometimes their efforts succeed in attracting her attention, and they form a stable partnership. But for many alpha females, the best solution to the aching desolation of living a solitary life in the middle of a pack is to find an alpha male from outside.

He may be a lone wolf traveling his own path, or the leader of a pack of his own. Either way, when these two passionate souls meet, sparks—and fur—usually fly!

RED IN TOOTH 

Sonja (Natassia Malthe) is the alpha female of the motorcycle pack in the movie *Skinwalkers* (2007). Fiercely loyal to her mate, she has fully embraced her dark nature, and is ruthless in her bid to live in a world without boundaries.

Chapter 4

Werewolves: Fact & Folklore

Science Versus Magic

NOW AND THEN

Modern science tells us that magic is illusory and that werewolves cannot and do not physically transform. But in former times things were not always so clear-cut.

When superstition ruled the courts, thousands of people were accused of the crime of werewolfism. Reaching a peak between 1520 and 1630, hundreds of innocent people were burned at the stake in an epidemic of popular paranoia. But being accused, and even convicted, does not always mean that the crime truly happened.

The importance of religion

It was a time when religion, not science, was the arbiter of truth, and the Christian scriptures were (despite their internal conflicts) the final word on every subject. Most theologians agreed that people couldn't physically change their human body into a wolf's body. It was, they thought, all an illusion—a trick played by the arch-trickster, the Devil and his minions—black magic, in fact.

Beyond science

Magic, by definition, is something mysterious, either deliberately hidden from the uninitiated, or simply too transcendental for words to express directly. Either way, magic is by its nature beyond the scope of science, and it is common sense to be sceptical and not accept magical claims at face value.

THE SCIENCE BEHIND THE TALES

However, science is constantly discovering new things, and there are many aspects of modern life that, even just a few centuries ago, would have been viewed as pure magic. So although the cause of certain effects may be as yet improperly understood, is that a good reason to dismiss them as impossible?

A question of interpretation

It is risky to accept evidence of events that are poorly observed, or whose interpretation is colored by bias. However, to ignore facts simply because they challenge your opinions is even more dangerous.

Suspend disbelief

So we may allow ourselves the luxury of suspending our disbelief for a short period of time, and enter into the spirit of explorers of the phenomenon.

As we confront the inexplicable, rather than dismissing it as unbelievable, we may ask ourselves instead "how could this possibly be true?" The conclusions may be confusing, but they may also be revealing.

Looking at stories

It is time to consider the ancient stories and modern folklore that tell us so much about the natural history of the werewolf—past and present.

Skinwalkers

"Skinwalking" means being in another creature's skin, not metaphorically or in a dream or trance, but as a physical reality. Incredible as it may sound, there is anecdotal evidence that such things really do happen, but few things seem more strange.

NATIVE AMERICAN TRADITION

Although the name could describe a wide range of transformation cases from around the world, the term "Skinwalker" specifically refers to a Native American tradition of the southwest of the United States, and is primarily associated with the Navajo tribe.

The unspoken

Because Skinwalkers are regarded as an aberration and evil, few members of those tribes who know about the phenomenon are willing to discuss it with anyone outside the community. So most "skinwalking" stories are like the following one, which involved people passing through a Native American reservation.

A MYSTERIOUS INCIDENT

The incident happened in the spellbinding environment of Monument Valley in the Navajo Indian Reservation, Arizona, about 25 miles (40 km) north of the small town of Kayenta. A family of four were driving home along Route 163 in the family pickup through a dark, moonless night in the summer of 1982 or 1983. There was thunder in the air, but the couple's two children, a young woman of 20 and her younger brother, were calm—the drive had been long and tiring.

Shock reactions

As the pickup approached a sharp bend in the road, the father slowed down as the shoulder of the road dipped steeply into a ditch. Suddenly the mother screamed and the father yelled, which made the boy start yelling, too. The daughter instinctively hammered down the door lock and grabbed the handle, bracing herself ready to hold it shut at all costs.

The father of the family had slammed on the breaks, almost bringing the vehicle to a stop as a figure leapt up out of the ditch toward the vehicle. Although he seemed to be wearing normal clothes, at least jeans and a shirt, this was no ordinary man: he appeared to be completely covered in black fur, like an animal dressed in a man's clothes.

Yellow eyes

The night was dark and nothing was visible outside the beams of the headlights, so as the creature approached the side of the cab, the father flicked on the interior bulb to shed a little extra light. Then they saw that whatever the creature was, its eyes were yellow. The father hit the gas and in the glow of the interior light the family could see how terrified he was: the hair on the back of his neck and his arms was sticking straight out.

Drumming

As if that ordeal wasn't enough, a few days later the children were awakened at home late at night by the sound of drumming coming from the forest behind the house. Looking from the boy's bedroom window they watched intently as the sound grew louder.

Several figures were approaching the low fence at the perimeter of the property. They looked humanoid, but when they tried to clamber over the fence they seemed unable to bring their legs up high enough. Finally giving up the attempt to reach the house, they began a dreadful chant, before melting away, back into the forest.

Pursuing power

When these events were mentioned to a family friend who was a Navajo, she told them that the creature on the road was a Skinwalker, a Navajo evil witch who had shape-shifted into the guise of an animal.

The friend was taken to view the fence, where she announced that the chanting figures were also Skinwalkers. They had tried to reach someone in the family because they wanted the power that the person possessed. Fortunately, a magical protection existed around the family, and that barrier had prevented the Skinwalkers from seizing their prey. The friend also expressed surprise that the Skinwalkers had visited, because they rarely menaced anyone outside their own Navajo community. In any case, she hadn't heard of any Skinwalkers being active for some years before then.

Comments invited

When this story was published, a website was set up a poll asking visitors to comment. Out of more than 8,000 replies, 56 percent said they believed the family had indeed encountered a real Skinwalker. Twenty-six percent said they did not believe it, while the remainder weren't sure.

Whether this straw poll is a useful measure of general belief in Skinwalkers, is open to question. Perhaps it simply tells us something about the people who read such articles on that website. With regards to whether this family actually came face to face with a Skinwalker, the jury is still out.

SKINWALKERS, THE TRADITION

Skinwalkers are, to use the common term, evil witches. They are poles apart from the traditional shamanic medicine man, and the distinction should be stressed.

WOLF ON THE WARPATH →

Like many Native American tribes, the Tuscarora have a wolf clan, membership of which is inherited through the mother. Traditionally, members are brothers and sisters in the clan and cannot intermarry. This 19th-century illustration depicts a Tuscarora warrior.

Identification

The most common animal that is selected by the Skinwalker is the wolf or the fearsome coyote, but smaller, more benign, animals such as foxes, and even birds, including owls and crows, are within the shape-shifting range.

Skinwalkers may be identified by their eyes, which can glow like red coals. Or, more subtly, when they are in animal form they can be identified because their eyes don't reflect light like the actual animal (the shining effect is caused by the *tapetum lucidum* behind the retina in the eye), yet when the Skinwalker is in human shape, conversely his eyes actually glow with reflected light, like an animal's.

On all-fours

The Navajo term for a Skinwalker is *yee naaldlooshii* or *yenaldlooshi*, which indicates traveling on all-fours (rather than two legs). As part of the ceremony that enables them to transform themselves, they often wear the skin of the creature they plan to become. Typically that is all they wear.

The animal is chosen for their particular purpose, perhaps to attack somebody, or maybe simply to hide their own human identity, but the usual intention is to be able to escape or travel with great agility and at great speed.

SKINWALKER OUTLAWS

As cultural deviants and predatory criminals, Skinwalkers are strictly outlawed by the Navajo. But because they use magic, which is a complex cultural motif that is as difficult to understand as it is easy to ridicule, they are rarely spoken of, particularly to people outside the community.

Mind-readers

Skinwalkers are also able to read minds, which enables them reputedly to use people's fears against them, not least of which is the idea that if you start talking about them too much, you'll attract their attention, and you'll get a visit you won't want repeated.

Unfortunately, of course, Skinwalkers thrive in secrecy, which allows them to rob, plunder, and plant spells to curse with bad luck, to maim, and to kill with impunity.

DEFENCES

Breaking such spells is an important part of the medicine man's role, but ceremonies to bless and protect a house can take up to a week to complete. First the spell must be found where the Skinwalker planted it, usually near the hogan (traditional Navajo earthen house); and then ritual must be used to destroy its power.

Beneficial practices

The Navajo Skinwalker may be tainted with evil nowadays, but the tradition probably grew out of beneficial shamanistic practices.

The Navajo were renowned as hunters, and their superb skills were the product of being able to "get inside the skull" of their prey, enabling them to predict the animal's whereabouts, and then anticipate its movements.

A Close Encounter

A traditional defence against a Skinwalker is publicly to announce his full name, after which the spell will rebound and afflict the witch himself.

Skinwalkers may also be killed by more conventional means, as is seemingly the case in this story.

A MYSTERIOUS FIGURE

Not long after sunset one evening sometime during 1980, some tourists from Indiana were driving through the Navajo Indian Reservation when a figure darted out of nowhere across the road in front of them.

They hit him, at speed, and when they stopped to try to assist him in any way they could, they discovered that he was dressed in animal pelts. He was also obviously dead.

SEEKING ADVICE

The accident happened near a small town and there were a few people present, but they wouldn't approach the body. Eventually the tourists drove off and, finding a small trading post near by, sought advice.

The trader sent them to the local police station, but wouldn't go with them. At the station they were kept waiting while their statements were taken and every detail was discussed, checked, and gone over.

NO TRACE

At last, the police captain seemed content, and he accompanied them to the scene of the accident. However, when they arrived they found that there was now no trace of the corpse.

The captain instantly dismissed the case, claiming the man had simply been knocked unconscious briefly and had fully recovered and gone home. He also insisted that the tourists should go on their way, and this is what they did.

BODY REMOVED

It appears that the local people had removed the body and deposited it in a natural depression, carefully covering it from sight. Then a powerful cleansing ceremony wiped away the residual evil the Skinwalker had left in its wake.

As it is a traditional Navajo right of self-defence to kill any Skinwalker they encounter, the local people must have felt the tourists had done them a favor.

The Lobizon

The Lobizon is a werewolf creature which is created automatically when a child is born who is the seventh son in a family that consists of sons and no daughters. Belief in the Lobizon is still very much alive today. The transformation is physical and is influenced by the phases of the Moon, with full Moon being the time of most transformations. Often, the Lobizon relishes their secret power and will taunt the victims whose livestock they have attacked.

THE SEVENTH SON

In past generations, belief in the damnation of the seventh son was so strong that these children were often abandoned or killed rather than see the family and community afflicted with a Lobizon. To counter this tradition, in the 1920s the president of Argentina became the official godfather-designate to these children. When they were baptized (often under the protective name Benito, meaning "Blessed") he became their godfather and gave them a gold medal and the state awarded them a scholarship until they were 21 years old. This stopped the curse inflicted on the seventh sons, but although the practice continues to this day, the Lobizon still looms large in the lives of the people.

DESTINATION TRUTH

In 2007 an episode of *Destination Truth* (also aired as *The Monster Hunter*) went in search of the Lobizon. Led by presenter Josh Gates, the team of six were investigating the Lobizon, for which there had recently been a spate of sightings in northern Argentina in locations as diverse as remote farmland and inner cities.

The team interviewed a man named Carlos, who claims to be a Lobizon and able to transform at will, and he volunteered to show them. In this case, although there was a clear transformation, it was only physical to the extent that any actor could produce.

Summoning the wolf

As he summoned the wolf from within himself he clutched his chest and looked around furtively. He started panting, his fingers going rigid and splayed like exaggerated claws. He bent over jerkily and sank onto all-fours, then knelt. He howled and the transformation was complete. It was also over, and he straightened up, checked his watch, and looked around to see what had been happening as he had no recollection of the events of the last few minutes.

Eyewitness

Another man, Jesus by name, claimed to be an eyewitness to a Lobizon. It happened in the early afternoon when he saw children throwing bricks at the creature. The Lobizon ran away, leaped up onto a cart, and then dashed into Jesus's house. Jesus lassoed the beast, dragged it outside, hit it several times with a big stick, and tied it up.

The Beast of Bray Road

Although often dubbed a werewolf, the "Wisconsin Wolfman"—the Beast of Bray Road—is often classified by cryptozoologists as a "cryptid": an ordinary animal that is so rare that its existence has yet to be formally established by science. The Beast was first sighted on a country road near Elkhorn, Wisconsin, USA, in the 1980s, and has been described as a large and intelligent wolf-like creature that roamed on its hind legs. While some people see this as being suspiciously bear-like, despite many investigations, the many sightings remain a mystery.

Author Linda S. Godfrey went on to research further anomalous animals in the USA in her book *Hunting the American Werewolf* (2006), which includes an update on the Beast of Bray Road, as well as an Anubis-headed creature haunting the Great Lakes.

Anubis was a god of Ancient Egypt who was associated with death and the afterlife: he had the head of a jackal and a form of a wild dog. Despite being located on the other side of the continent, this creature was described as a "Skinwalker" (see page 119).

However, when his back was turned the Lobizon broke free and escaped. The lasso, Josh noticed, was covered in blood.

Being the night of the full Moon, the team hung up a side of beef (the Lobizon is known to eat raw meat) and set up surveillance cameras. They caught a fleeting glimpse of an animal, later identified as the maimed wolf. Coincidence? The lasso that had reportedly been bloodied by the captured creature identified as a Lobizon was taken for DNA testing at the forensic laboratory of the University of California. The blood was compared with their database, and found to be 100 percent human.

CRYPTOZOOLOGY

The study of secretive creatures, or hidden animals as the word cryptozoology means, embraces a very broad field of interest. Most activity ranges from investigating sightings of extremely rare species not yet cataloged by science, such as the yeti or the Loch Ness monster, to finding ordinary animals in unexpected places such as the big cats of Britain (thought to be escaped or released panthers). But at the outer edge of this fringe subject, discreetly labeled "Here be monsters," live the outright bizarre creatures such as the fire-breathing dragon and the shape-shifter. This wonderful menagerie offers a comfortable niche for the werewolf.

British Werewolves

The "lack" of werewolves in Britain seems extraordinary in a country so famous for its rich variety of other paranormal activity, but may be related to the early annihilation of the wolf population, which was decimated by King Edgar in the 10th century. Their extermination was ordered by Edward I in 1281, although some small pockets survived in remote areas, and total extinction in all parts of the British Isles was not complete until around 1760. These days there are plans to reintroduce wolves back into the wilds in some carefully monitored locations.

A remarkably similar set of sightings, however, did occur in Britain, and this has been claimed as one of the country's very few werewolf stories.

Sightings

In his book *Haunted Liverpool 3* (1998), Tom Slemen writes of how, in 2002, a sheep farmer reported seeing a large bear-like creature that had killed his lambs on the night of the full Moon. Numerous similar cryptids were seen in the area around the same time, which soon got people recalling events from two hundred years before. According to Elliott O'Donnell (*Werwolves,* 1912) a wolf-headed man was said to haunt the Valley of the Doones, Exmoor, UK.

In 1790 a stagecoach had been attacked on the Denbigh to Wrexham route. It was dusk, with a full Moon rising, when a black beast leaped on one of the horses, which was pulling the coach, and killed it. The creature was described as being the same size as the horse.

Paw prints

In the winter of the following year prodigious paw prints were found in the snow a few miles to the east of Gresford, seemingly belonging to an enormous wolf. Following the tracks led to a field of slaughtered livestock. The farmer himself was found barricaded into his own home, having seen the huge, black, wolf-like creature in its killing spree. The blue-eyed beast tried to batter down his door and walked around to peer through his windows, standing on its hind legs like a person. Church leaders added a spiritual, or rather a demonic, ingredient to the terror that stalked the rural community, by branding the ravening creature as a werewolf. Despite many searches, it was never found.

THE WOLF AT THE DOOR

In the harshest of Winters, when normal prey is impossible to find or has been driven away by encroaching farmers, wolves may be driven to attack humans. This 19th-century wood engraving depicts wolves attacking settlers in a remote part of Illinois, USA.

Circe the Enchantress

A DEVELOPING PICTURE

Having heard some modern accounts of werewolves, let us reach back through time to the beginning. Starting from the oldest records we can build up a picture of the development of the phenomenon, from classical myth to courtly romances, and from medieval religious mania to the wisdom of folktales. Probably the most ancient description of werewolves comes from Homer. *The Odyssey*, tells the story of Odysseus, a hero of the Trojan War, and how he journeyed for ten years and experienced many adventures, to find his way home.

Wolves and lions

Odysseus notices smoke coming from the heart of the forest, and the men in his party draw lots to see who should investigate. A band of 23 set out, finding a building of polished stone, to their horror, surrounded by mountain wolves and lions.

These lions and strong-clawed wolves start to run at the men, who are terrified by their size and powerful jaws, but the beasts do not attack. Instead, they approach with wagging tails and prancing gait, and fawn like neglected pets. These creatures were once men who had ventured into the house of the beautiful yet dreadful goddess Circe, and she had turned them all into werewolves and were-lions. They now have the bodies of beasts and the wits of men; and they are all hungry for human companionship.

Beckoning

But the wolves cannot speak to communicate their knowledge, and all the while, from within the house, comes the sweet, beckoning song of a woman, a goddess—Circe. She greets them and prepares a meal for them, but in it she has concealed a drug that makes them forget their own homes; and with a stroke of her wand she transforms them into swine. Their minds are still their own, but Circe casts them outdoors to join the wolves and lions in her nightmare collection of were-creatures.

Only one man escapes, and he returns to the ship and tells Odysseus. The hero sets out to rescue his men and he meets the god Hermes, who gives him a herb called "moly," whose root is black and whose flower is white—the countermeasure to Circe's poisonous drug.

Odysseus is welcomed by Circe and she prepares him a drink in a golden cup. In this she puts her ruinous drug. He drains the cup and Circe strikes him with her wand, consigning him to the pigsty. But Odysseus is not transformed; the magic herb from Hermes has worked like the charm it is. Now, Odysseus springs on her with his naked sword. Having met her match, Circe sees Odysseus through new eyes, and she finds him instantly attractive. She invites him to her bed. First he insists that she swears an oath not to harm him, which she is happy enough to do.

The heroes depart

Having sampled her hospitality, Odysseus remembers his shipmates and, at his simple request, Circe frees all of them. She anoints each with a potion that returns them to human form and restores memories of homes and families. It also makes them younger-looking and more handsome than before.

Becoming a myth

Then the heroes sail away and leave Circe, and her sad companions the werewolves and were-lions, in their forest grove on the enchanted isle—receding into the remoteness of myth.

MISTRESS OF ANIMALS

In this watercolor, "Circe Pouring Poison into a Vase and Awaiting the Arrival of Ulysses" (1863–9) by Edward Burne-Jones, one of the greatest Pre-Raphaelite painters, Circe prepares the potion she will use to turn Odysseus (also known as Ulysses) into a beast. The lions at her feet were earlier victims.

Fabulous Wolves in Fables

Fables, in which animals enjoy human characteristics, such as the ability to speak, are often dismissed in the same breath as fairytales as being "just for children," but that is to do them an injustice. They are worth having a closer look at, as we shall see.

SUBJECTS OF STUDY

Socrates, the famous Greek philosopher (literally "lover of wisdom") is said to have formed one of Aesop's fables into verse while awaiting his own execution. Demetrius of Phalerum, the librarian of the vast Library of Alexandria, was also an ardent collector of Aesop's fables. Such men did not waste time on fancies, but found fables to be worthy subjects of study.

Fabulous creatures

Their reputation as "nonsense fit only for the nursery" stems from an overly mechanistic view of the world in which talking animals were viewed as absurd and irrational. Indeed any such impossible creature could be described (and written off) as fabulous, literally as if it belonged in a fable.

Original meaning

Curiously, the modern use of that word has evolved to mean something wonderful, which is rather closer to the original meaning, because fables were stories that tried to explain something that was really inexplicable.

Accurate personality traits

Many fables are ancient, so many of the topics they discuss no longer seem mysterious to us, but it is also startling how accurately the animals satirize personality traits that are as common and conspicuous today as they were in days gone by.

The simple moral lessons that may be drawn from fables are also of enduring value, and this has ensured their survival as adults appreciated the educational slant, while children simply treasured the marvelous stories.

AESOP'S FABLES

The following selection of Aesop's fables portrays the wolf with human speech and reasoning. The first is an amusing variant on the idea of the wolf in human guise.

THE WOLF IN SHEEP'S CLOTHING

A cunning wolf tries unsuccessfully to get close enough to a docile flock of sheep to capture one for his dinner.

A simple disguise

He finds the skin of a sheep that has been butchered by the shepherd, with its skin left behind. The wolf carefully takes the skin and puts it on over his own pelt, then strolls down to where the flock is grazing. Disguised in this way, it is a simple thing for him to approach a sheep and seize it before he is noticed.

Aesop

Aesop, whose collection is world renowned, is thought to have lived in Greece in the 6th century BCE. He may, as one early account insists (*The Book of Xanthus the Philosopher and his Slave Aesop*), have been a slave owned by a philosopher, and who was able to rebut his master's complex and sophisticated theories with his own simple, earthy wit, captured in his fables.

Some people, though, think Aesop did not actually exist, but was simply a convenient nom-de-plume for anonymous writers and editors who wrote and collected fables that had already been circulating for centuries by word of mouth.

Either way, these ancient fables are a unique literary take on the werewolf, and reveal a fascinating portrait of the wolf with human characteristics.

The most famous of all fables about a wolf requires mentioning simply because it is so well-known. It's the story of the boy who cried wolf: he was a shepherd's boy and several times raised the alarm, calling men from the village to save the flock from predation. Each time they arrived he laughed at them. A wolf was attracted by the commotion, but when the boy called for help, the men shrugged it off and ignored the yells, as the wolf enjoyed his supper.

THE WOLVES AND THE SHEEP

A pack of wolves addresses a flock of sheep, speaking to them with cunning diplomacy, "Why is there always fear and bloodshed between us?" they ask, "It's all the fault of those wicked dogs. They bark at us all the time, and attack us before we can get close enough to you. If you send them away, there could be peace and reconciliation between us and you." The sheep think that this sounds reasonable and they dismiss the dogs there and then. The wolves feast well upon the flock that night!

THE WOLF AND THE LAMB

A wolf wants to convince a lamb of his right to eat it. He says sternly, "You insulted me last year." But the lamb replies that it had not been born then. The wolf says accusingly, "You eat in my pasture." But the lamb replies that it had not yet eaten grass. The wolf says reproachfully, "You drink from my water hole." But the lamb says it hasn't tasted water either, just milk from its mother. Then the wolf eats the lamb, and says afterward, "Never mind. I couldn't convince you, but I'm not going hungry just for that!"

THE DOG AND THE WOLF

A working dog is out walking when he meets a starving wolf by the side of the road. The dog speaks to his cousin, the wolf, and comments that the wolf's way of life is obviously too irregular to be healthy. He invites the wolf along to find a steady job.

Bare patch

The wolf feels at a low ebb, and replies, "I have no objection to that." So they go off together to find the dog's master and get the wolf a job. While on the way, the wolf notices a bare patch of skin on the dog's neck.

The dog says it that this is where his master puts a collar on him at night to keep him chained securely at home. He admits that it hurts a bit, but adds that you soon get used to it. To this the wolf replies, "Indeed, I see. Then good-bye Sir Dog!" The wolf goes back, alone.

THE WOLVES AND THE SHEEPDOGS

The wolves speak to the sheepdogs saying, "You are like us in so many ways, why don't you live with us in peace, as brothers? The only difference between us is that we are free, while you cower down in servitude to men who beat you and chain you in collars."

Agreement

"You guard all their sheep, yet they eat them and give you mere bones to chew. You should join us and we will feast together on all the sheep we want." The dogs agree with this appraisal and are glad to be welcomed into the wolf den. There, the dogs are slaughtered.

THE WOLF AND THE SHEPHERDS

A wolf is passing a hut in which some shepherds are quietly enjoying their dinner of mutton. "What a fuss you'd make," the wolf says to them, "if you saw me doing what you're doing!"

THE NURSE AND THE WOLF

A nurse, impatient with a crying child, tells it to stop its noise or she'll feed it to the wolves. As chance would have it, a hungry wolf is passing the house, and hears this.

He blesses his luck, and sits under the window, waiting for an easy meal, as he is sure the obnoxious child will start wailing again soon.

No trust

As the dreadful noise starts up again the wolf wags its tail, yelps with joy, and opens its jaws in anticipation. But the nurse slams the window shut and calls out the dogs to set upon the wolf. "Typical," thinks the wolf as he runs away. "You just can't trust your enemies."

WOLF IN SHEPHERD'S CLOTHING 

In this engraving—"The Wolf Turned Shepherd"—from the 1867 edition of *Fontaine's Fables*, Gustave Doré presents a memorable image of the power and peril of disguise. Such cautionary tales have an enduring relevance that is best learned at an early age.

Myths & Legends

THE WOLF-TYRANT OF ARCADIA

Arcadia was, and still is, something of a byword for the utopian pastoral lifestyle, where time idles by in merriment and love.

Located in the heart of the Peloponnese peninsula of southern Greece, it is a mountainous region with little military or political significance.

Natural setting

It remained relatively untroubled by the wars of the more civilized tribes in the Mediterranean. As something of a cultural backwater, where a primitive way of life survived, and about which little was known, it was the natural setting for tales of eldritch lore and primal magic.

The Arcadia of myth became populated by a host of otherworldly beings, including the werewolf, and was ruled by the anarchic god Pan. Arcadia has been likened to the irrational, even surreal, realm of the subconscious mind, whose profoundly symbolic inhabitants wield powerful magic over our dreams and waking emotions.

Lycaon

But the perception of a place often differs from the reality—one of their earliest kings, the infamous tyrant, Lycaon, was a werewolf. According to *Pseudo-Apollodorus*, Lycaon was the grandson of Zeus. Despite, or perhaps because of this high ancestry, Lycaon's sons were so selfish that Zeus sent the great flood to cleanse the world of them and their like.

ALSO IN ARCADIA

In the eighth of his *Eclogues,* which extol the Arcadian idyll, the poet Virgil mentions herbs brought from Pontus (the south coast of the Black Sea) that can change a man into a werewolf. Wisely, perhaps, he does not name them.

The Roman author Pliny the Elder (c.23–79) wrote an encyclopedic *Natural History (Historia Naturalis)* in which he discusses a range of subjects varying from astronomy to mining, with a wealth of natural and supernatural topics in between. In *Book Eight,* he touches on the subject of werewolves.

Family sacrifice

He quotes the source of the popular belief as being a Greek author Euanthes, who recorded the

THE MURDEROUS MAN–WOLF

The monstrous Lycaon is depicted here with his head transformed into that of a wolf—clearly revealing his state of mind. He is seen on his way to kill his guest, little knowing that it is the god Zeus in disguise. This engraving (1523) is by the Italian Renaissance artist Agostino de Musi.

·M·D· XXIII
·A·V·

Roman Tales of Lycaon

The Roman poet Ovid (43 BCE–c.18 AD) writes of Lycaon's evil in *Metamorphoses.* He tells how Zeus has traveled to the mortal realm, passed through the pinewoods of Mount Lycaeus, and arrives at the court of Lycaon, the king, as night falls.

Zeus gives signs of his divinity, and many of the Arcadian people understand and are reverent toward him, but Lycaon is disbelieving and dismissive; and he plots to slay the charismatic stranger as he sleeps.

Zeus, of course, does not fall for that trick. But Lycaon tries another deception—he murders a prisoner and cooks his flesh, serving it as a meal for his unwelcome guest.

The king of the gods is incandescent with rage, and instantly burns the palace to the ground. Lycaon flees in terror into the fields, where he howls in anguish. He starts foaming at the mouth and, with his vengeful heart still thirsty for blood, he attacks a flock of the sheep. Devouring the animals, his clothes become bristling fur, his arms become legs, and he becomes a wolf. Only the gray of his human hair remains in his pelt, and the savagery in his glittering eyes remains recognizable as Lycaon.

The Greek traveler Pausanias records a different version of the tale in his *Description of Greece* written around the year 170. He says Lycaon goes to Mount Lycaeus, where Zeus had been born. There, at the god's temple, King Lycaon offers a human baby as a sacrifice.

However, Zeus does not accept the sacrifice and, as the baby's blood pools on the altar, he transforms Lycaon into a wolf. Ever since, anyone who offers a sacrifice at the temple of Zeus Lycaeus also turns into a werewolf. But, so long as they do not taste human flesh, the curse is lifted after nine years, and they can return to human form. Lycaon himself lived as a wolf for the rest of his life.

Although there are points of disagreement between the various writers regarding exactly how, why, when, and even whether King Lycaon was doomed to live the life of a wolf, this ancient story has been cherished for centuries by students of werewolf lore. However, the fact that the tale clearly evolved as it passed through the hands of different writers spanning many generations, is a caution to us all against accepting folklore at face value. Even so, the fascinating prospect of finding truth at the source of these tales keeps them the subject of lively discussion.

story told by the Arcadians. They said that a member of the family of Anthus is periodically selected by lot and taken to a particular marsh with a stretch of open water. There, the man hangs his clothes on an oak tree, swims across the water, and wanders to a deserted place. He then physically changes into a wolf and lives as a member of the local wolf pack for nine years.

Regain human shape

On condition that he has not had contact with humans during his stay with the wolves, after nine years the werewolf will return to the marsh, swim across, and regain his human shape. His clothes will be found secure where he left them on the oak tree.

Pliny the Elder dismisses the idea that human beings can physically turn into wolves, saying it is in the same class of fabulous notions that, over the course of many generations, have all been determined to be untrue.

Popular belief

He does, however, accept that belief in werewolves was currently popular, and was called *versipellis* or "changing the skin," and that many people regarded the sufferer as being under a very real curse.

Pliny was derisive about this legend, and quipped that even the most impossible thing can always find a witness to support it. It is ironic, therefore, that Pliny believed in a great many of the things mentioned in his *Natural History* that are, by today's reckoning, equally impossible.

ROMULUS AND REMUS

The myth of Romulus and Remus is the most famous story about children raised by wolves. The Roman historian Livy (c.59 BCE—17 AD) tells their story in his monumental work *The History of Rome* (Books One and Four).

Born in captivity

Mars, the Roman god of agriculture and war, forces his love upon Rea Silvia, a Vestal Virgin, and she becomes pregnant. The raped priestess is punished with imprisonment and her twin boys are born in captivity in or around 771 BCE. The king, who fears the children might one day seize his throne, orders that they are to be drowned in the River Tiber.

Left to die

The river, however, is flooding, and the deep channel cannot be reached, so the infants are left to die of exposure beside a fig tree at the water's edge. Their cries attract the attention of a she-wolf, who has come to the river to drink.

She is a gentle creature, who has recently given birth herself, and she suckles the children, caring for them as if they are her own cubs. Eventually a shepherd comes along and takes the children home to his wife.

Misinterpretation

Livy doubts the tradition of the wolf saving the children, as it seemed so implausible. He voices instead the idea that the legend arose from a simple misinterpretation. The term "she-wolf" (lupa), he notes, was commonly used to denote a prostitute, and perhaps the shepherd's wife bore the nickname (removing the actual wolf from the story). However, with the numbers of documented cases of wolf children across the centuries (see page 36), it does not seem impossible that a real she-wolf did in fact adopt the babies.

LUPERCALIA

Traditionally, Lupa, the she-wolf, carries the twins Romulus and Remus gently in her jaws into the shelter of her cave. This cave became known as the "Lupercal," and was on the Palatine Hill, upon which Rome was originally founded (by Romulus, having killed his brother) in or around 753 BCE. The cave was associated with the Lupercalia, the Festival of the Wolf, held each year between the 13th and 15th of February.

Festival of shepherds

Despite its name, the Lupercalia was primarily a festival of shepherds, and was held in honor of Faunus (Roman cognate of the Greek god Pan, worshiped as Pan Lycaon in Arcadia) whose statue stood in the Lupercal. After the sacrifice of a dog and two goats, and after a feast, the goatskins were cut into strips.

Ancient ritual

The Luperci (Brothers of the Wolf) took off all their clothes, and tied one thong of goatskin around themselves as a girdle or belt, and took another in hand. Otherwise naked, these men ran right around the perimeter of the old city wall, a route lined with cheering girls and women. The men used the second strip of goatskin to whip the women, who vied for attention from the Luperci. The underlying significance of this ancient pagan ritual lay in the belief that the women, touched by the primal god's powers, would have an easy time becoming pregnant, and be assured of a safe and swift delivery at childbirth.

Still popular

The Christian Church secured the closure of pagan temples and sanctuaries in AD 391, and it frowned upon all public events that were of a pagan nature. However, the Lupercalia was so popular that it was still celebrated more than a century later.

EARLY IRISH WEREWOLVES

The Church, it seems, is responsible for much of the werewolf population in Ireland. According to the mid 13th-century Norse book *Kongs Skuggsko*, the proselytizing Saint Patrick faced one particular tribe of Celtic pagans, who so heckled and jeered at him, and tried to howl him down, that he became angry and asked God to punish them. And so he did.

MOTHER WOLF

This legendary moment as the she-wolf suckles the twins Romulus and Remus, offers a fresh perspective on the human–wolf equation. The children experience a wildness beyond human motherliness, while the wolf is seen at its most passive; maternal and humane.

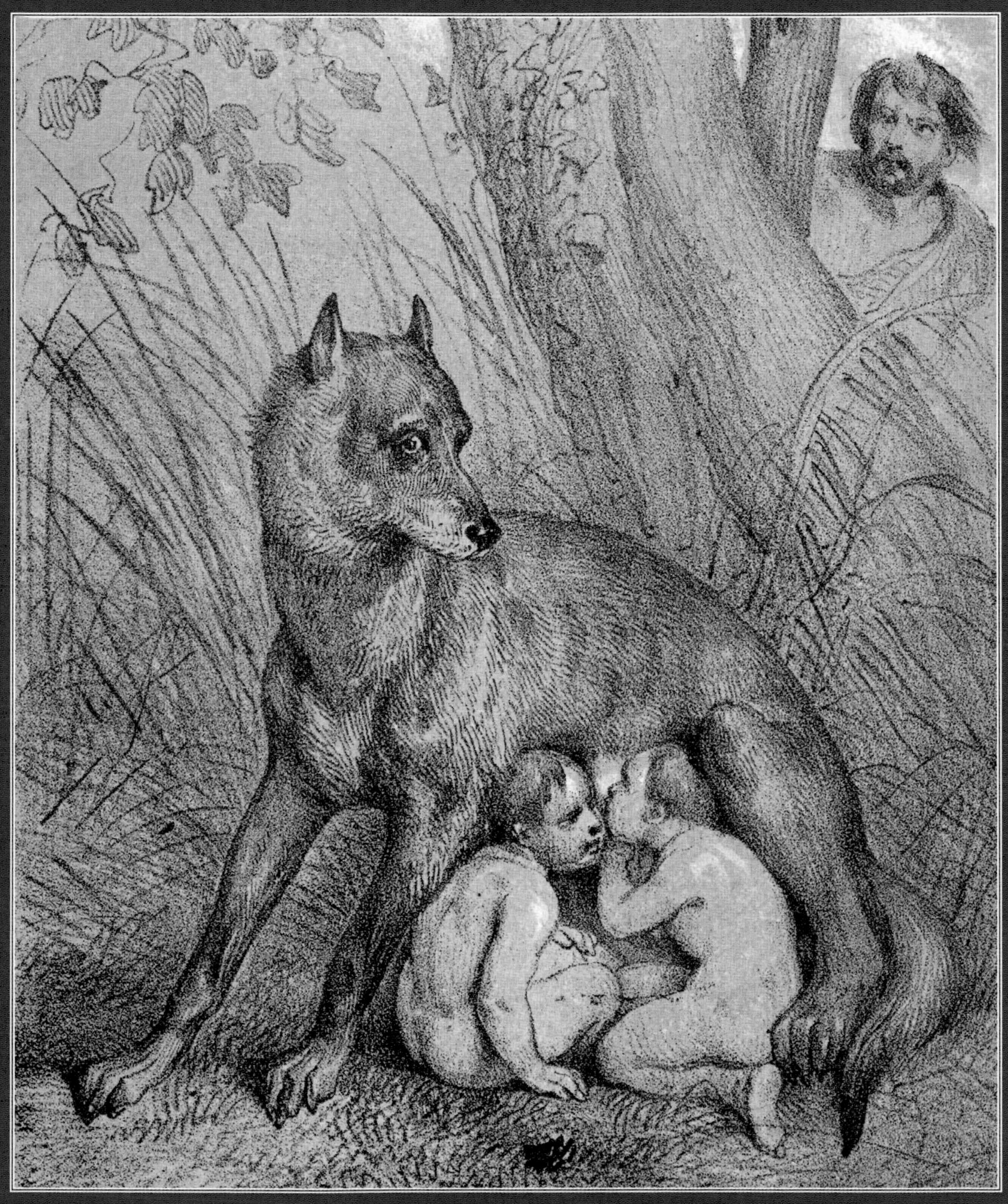

Dining With a Werewolf

Whether any such relic of ancient wisdom survives in the following story, is very much open to question: it appears in the *Satyricon* (Book 15, 61) a book renowned for its bawdy humor. It was written in the 1st century by Petronius, who was a favorite of the infamous Roman emperor Nero. The tale is told by Niceros, an ex-slave, at a dinner party part-hosted by his friend Trimalchio.

He tells of a brilliantly moonlit walk to see his lover, Melissa, who has been widowed that very day, making it an irreverently joyful occasion. Niceros is accompanied partway on this walk by one of his house guests, who happens to be a stout soldier.

Having walked for some distance through the night, they come to a place where tombs are sited alongside the road. Unexpectedly, the soldier leaves the road and heads straight in among the tombs. Niceros finds a convenient tomb to sit on and whistles while he waits for the soldier to finish what is, presumably, a call of Nature.

To Niceros's astonishment, however, the soldier strips naked, carefully piles his clothes by the side of the road and urinates in a ring around them. Then he turns into a wolf, howls, and runs off into the woods.

Niceros approaches the clothes to tidy them more safely, but they have turned to stone. Terrified, he hastens onward and arrives at his lover's home, staring blankly like a ghost, gasping for breath, and pouring with sweat. But Melissa is untroubled by his appearance, shrugging it off, saying what a pity it is he hadn't arrived earlier, when he could have been helpful. A wolf has attacked their livestock, and has been seen off by a slave stabbing its neck with a spear.

A nervous wreck, Niceros stays with Melissa until daylight, and then races away homeward. As he passes the tombs he finds only bloodstains where the soldier's clothes had been. Reaching home he finds the soldier lying in bed, with a physician attending to a gash in his neck.

Niceros realizes he is a man who can change his skin (a "versipellis"), and he can never stomach dining in the man's presence again.

Retaining a human mind

In retaliation for having howled like wolves, each male member of the tribe is cursed to turn into a wolf, yet retain their human minds and memory. Some of them turn into a werewolf for one year every seven years, while others spend seven years running wild in the woods, hunting with bare teeth and claws, before returning to human form, never to change again.

The Irish version of the *Historia Britonum of Nennius* mentions the descendents of the wolf at Ossory, in central Ireland in the province of Leinster. It echoes a 13th-century poem on the

"Wonders of Ireland" that describes how this clan can leave their own bodies at will, and take on the form of wolves. Sheep are said to be their favorite prey, which fall defenceless before them; but the transformation is not without risk to the people. They are not only vulnerable to being hurt while in their wolf form, as any injury to the wolf will be repeated on their human bodies, but if their human bodies are moved—however slightly—they will be unable to return into them, and be doomed to remain as wolves for the rest of their lives.

NORSE WEREWOLVES

The ancient Icelandic story of the death of King Siggeir of Stigny includes an incident with two werewolves. It circulated widely in the Middle Ages, and its earliest version is told in the *Volsunga Saga,* written around 1400 from an older tradition of spoken poetry. It came to English-speaking audiences translated as *The Story of the Volsungs* (1888).

Under a spell

Sigmund and Sinfjotli, who is Sigmund's son—but neither knows that they are related—are venturing through a great wood when they chance upon a house. Inside they find two sleeping men who are under a spell. For nine days they are wolves, and on the tenth they can take off the enchanted wolf-skins and rest as the men they once were.

Wolf form

Sigmund and Sinfjotli, eager for adventure, steal the wolf-skins and put them on. Instantly the spell of the wolf-skins binds them to wolf form. They howl just like wolves and they both understand the language of the wolf. They make a pact to go their separate ways, yet come to the other's aid should either of them be set upon by more than seven men.

When Sigmund meets some hunters who seek to kill him, he howls the wolf's call, and Sinfjotli comes to his side at once. Together the two werewolves slay all the men.

When Sinfjotli is attacked by 11 hunters he slays them all by himself and rests beneath an oak. Sigmund comes by and asks why he didn't call him for aid. His son simply says he needs no help in killing so few men.

An insult

Sigmund takes that quip badly, as an insult to his own prowess, for he had asked for aid when faced with far fewer foes. Sigmund rushes at Sinfjotli, making him stagger and fall, and bites him in the throat. Sinfjotli doesn't get up.

Repenting, both of his rage against the boy and of their folly in putting on the wolf-skins, Sigmund carries Sinfjotli back to the house in the wood (for the two other men, released from their curse, have gone back to their homes).

Two weasels

Then Sigmund sees two weasels fighting, and one bites the other's throat, then the victor runs into a thicket and returns with a leaf that it puts to the wound. Straight away the wounded weasel revives as fit as before.

Hier fiötra ÆSIR Fenris:
Ulfinn: Tÿr misser syna adra:
Hönd: en þr Aristera Ulfinn til Ra:
gna Röckurs: so sem XXIX Eddu
Dæmisaga Utvÿsar.

A raven

Sigmund goes in search of the healing herb himself, but as he does so he sees a raven bearing a sprig to him. He takes it and puts it to the wound on Sinfjotli's throat. Straight away the younger wolf revives, fit as before.

As soon as the tenth day arrives and they can return to human form, they build a fire and burn the wolf-skins to ashes.

ODIN

Another Icelandic manuscript, the *Codex Regius* (1270), includes the prophesy that Odin, chief of the Norse gods, will be killed by the great wolf Fenrir, who finally breaks free of his chains at the time of *Ragnarok* (Destiny of the Gods). Odin himself has two wolves, one called Geri (Greedy) and the other Freki (Ravenous) and they accompany him into the final battle.

THE BERSERKERS

The infamous Norse warrior-class, called the Berserkers, were characterized by the bloodthirsty rage that gave them the strength of many men.

RESTRAINING THE BEAST 

In Norse legend Fenrir, the wolf, grows so fearfully large that the gods make a magic leash. Suspecting a trap, Fenrir demands that one of the gods place his hand between his jaws, only then will he submit to try the leash for a while. It is, of course, permanent, and the god Tyr loses his right hand.

Invincible

They invoked the powers of the indomitable alpha wolf into themselves like a battle-frenzy, making them all but invincible. One such gang, the Ulfhethnar, wore the skins of wolves over their heads when they wished to "go berserk," and hailed Odin as their god. Other Berserkers were devoted to the bear, but each used the power of animal transformation to become something other than human.

A FRENCH ROMANCE

An early French romance (c.1200) that cautions us against an automatic dread of werewolves was written by one of the few women writers of werewolf fiction—Marie of France. Although her precise identity is not known for sure, she was certainly familiar with courtly life, both in France and England.

The title of her lay, or narrative song *Bisclavret,* is the Breton word for werewolf. It tells the tale of a great and gallant lord of Brittany, a friend of the king, who although greatly loved and respected, has a dark secret. Each week, for the space of three days, he leaves his devoted wife, and disappears into the countryside.

An explanation

Eventually she persuades him to explain. On those days, he says, he becomes a werewolf and hunts in the woods for his food. To change, he takes off his clothes and hides them under a stone beneath a bush beside an old chapel; he hides them carefully because without them he cannot revert to human form.

Werewolf in the Court of King Arthur

There is a mention of a werewolf in *Le Morte D'Arthur* by Sir Thomas Mallory. Despite its chivalrous subject—King Arthur, the Knights of the Round Table, and the Holy Grail—Mallory actually finished writing it while he was in prison, in 1469. Nevertheless, it was one of the first books to be printed in England (published by William Caxton in 1485), and was so popular it became influential as a benchmark of morality.

A GOOD KNIGHT

The werewolf story relates to Sir Marrok, but all we are told is that he is a good knight who had been betrayed by his wife, who turned him into a werewolf—an affliction that lasts for seven years. How she accomplishes her curse, or why she betrayed him, we are not informed, nor even how he found a cure.

Sir Marrok is mentioned in passing, as one of 110 knights who try to cure the bleeding wounds of another knight. Sir Urre receives seven grievous wounds in a fair fight in which he slays his opponent. The defeated knight's mother is a sorceress, and she uses her subtle crafts to cause Sir Marrok's wounds to alternately bleed and fester; they shall never be healed except by the ministrations of the very best knight in the world. Sir Marrok is positioned sixth from the last of the 110 knights who tried and failed to heal Sir Urre, a list that is headed by King Arthur himself.

Ultimately, it is the arrival of Sir Lancelot who prays, cleans the wounds, and enables the curse to be broken. Under Sir Lancelot's hands, the gashes on Sir Urre's body close immediately, and look as though they have been healed for a full seven years.

KNIGHT MELION

The knight Melion, whose story is told in the 13th-century Breton *Lai de Melion*, is transformed into a wolf when his wife touches him on the head with the stone of her magical ring. As he scampers off chasing a stag, she turns and runs away with the squire. Melion tracks them down, however, and when King Arthur discovers her treachery she uses the ring again, and returns him to human form.

ARTHUR AND GORLAGON

In *Arthur and Gorlagon* King Arthur hears another tale of wifely infidelity. Here, the husband is turned into a wolf by being struck on the head with the trunk of a shrub that has sprouted on the day he was born. A second stroke returns him to humanity.

Unwelcome news

His wife, although she has been previously happy in her life with her lord, is stricken to the heart by this news, and love soon withers in her breast, and dies. Her dread of him is such that she can no longer abide to go to his bed, and her life becomes intolerable.

An old admirer

As chance would have it a knight, an old admirer, is passing and renews his acquaintance with her. She sees an opportunity to rid herself of her problem and start a new life.

She confides in this knight and the next time her lord slips away from the castle, the knight follows him and steals his clothes. Despite a search, the people are not surprised that their lord, who so often vanished before, had now disappeared. In due course the "widow" marries her knight, whose patience, and a little theft, had brought down the lord.

Like a faithful dog

A full year later, the king goes hunting to the very woods where the stranded bisclavret lives, and the king's hounds corner him. But when the bisclavret sees his old friend, the king, he is overjoyed and bounds forward and puts a paw to his stirrup, greeting the king like a faithful dog.

The king, marveling at this unheard-of behavior, calls off the hounds and takes the wolf home to his castle. The king and his wolf become inseparable. One day the king calls all his knights to his castle, and among them is the knight that stole the lord's clothes. As soon as the bisclavret sees him he bounds forward with bared teeth, and would have killed him had the king not restrained him. The knight departs as soon as the meetings are over.

Overnight

Once again, the king goes hunting in the wood where they found the bisclavret, and he stays in a lodge overnight. Next morning he receives a visit from the knight's wife, and again the wolf turns savage, leaping up and biting her nose right off.

This recurrence of vicious behavior nearly results in the wolf's death, as it seems he is turning wild, but a wise man raises his voice and counsels restraint. He declares that these events are beyond coincidence, noting that the woman is the wife of the knight, and was the wife of the lord who disappeared in this very wood.

A confession

The king seizes the knight and his wife, and under more than the threat of torture, she confesses to her treacherous act. She brings the clothes out of hiding and they are put in a room with the wolf and left for a while. When the king ventures in he finds his old friend, the lord, asleep on the bed, and wakens him to a joyous revival of camaraderie.

Exiled together

The lord's werewolfism is counted a trifle compared with his wife's monstrous abandonment of her love and duty toward him. She and her knight are exiled together.

WILLIAM AND THE WEREWOLF

The English poem, popularly known as *William and the Werewolf,* was originally entitled *The Romance of William of Palerne,* and was translated into English in about 1350 from the immensely popular twelfth-century French romance.

Powerful ointment

It tells the tale of Alphonsus, the heir to the Spanish throne, who is turned into a werewolf by his jealous stepmother, Braunde. Through her knowledge of the Black Arts she concocts a powerful ointment. When she anoints Alphonsus with it he turns into a wolf, yet still retains his human wits.

Under the enchantment, the werewolf Alphonsus snatches an infant from Palermo in Sicily and swims with the boy to mainland Italy. This is not just any child, however; he is William, the king's son. The wolf nurtures William and raises him as best he can, but while the werewolf is out hunting for food, a cowherd discovers the child, and he adopts him.

When Alphonsus discovers that William is safe, he leaves the child with the cowherd and his wife. But William's life as a cowherd's son is not destined to last.

The lost emperor

One day the Emperor of Rome is out hunting, but becomes separated from his companions and finds himself lost. He meets William and is so impressed with the boy that he takes him back to court on the back of his own horse, and appoints him as pageboy to his daughter Melior.

William and Melior fall in love and elope. The lovers wander deep into the forest, and make themselves a den, but are threatened with starvation until Alphonsus, the werewolf, chances to find them. He goes hunting, robs some travelers, and returns with food and wine. With his constant support, they reach Sicily.

Heraldic device

William's father, the king, is dead, so William leads the fight to save their kingdom from the invading King of Spain. When William's mother asks what heraldic device he wishes to be painted on his shield, he describes a startling design:

"By Christ, madam, I desire nothing else
but that I have a good shield clad in clean gold,
and well and fairly depicted on it—a werewolf
that is hideous and huge, with all his correct
and most suitable color, so to be obvious in the
field (of battle); other (coat of) arms, in all my life
I'll never have."

A MATTER OF LIFE AND DEATH →

A werewolf has snatched a child and now flees, closely pursued by an armed man. While clearly wolf-like, this werewolf is bipedal and clothed. This illustration is from a woodcut dated 1832.

His efforts are rewarded with success, both military and romantic. And, with the King of Spain captured, his wife Braunde releases Alphonsus from the spell that had bound him in the form of a wolf. She is pardoned for her crime, and it is revealed that Alphonsus had not maliciously stolen young William, but had actually bravely rescued him in the nick of time from being murdered.

Restoration

So, the faithful werewolf, Alphonsus, is restored to princely human form, and restored to his rightful place as heir to the Spanish throne, and is also exonerated of his questionable motives in taking the young William. Perhaps even more importantly, he and William's sister Florence fall in love and they share the wedding celebration with William and Melior.

CAMP OF THE DOG

The spirit that can depart from the body and prowl abroad, with physical strength and fierce intent, is the theme that inspired the prolific writer of supernatural tales, Algernon Blackwood, to write his classic werewolf story *Camp of the Dog* (1908). It is a remarkable tale that is a celebration of love, yet is also a warning about the terrible spiritual danger that may arise when the path of true love is blocked. But, of course, this short summary is no substitute for reading the full narrative.

The story

To the north of Stockholm, Sweden, are innumerable islands set like jewels in the Baltic Sea, and among the most remote of these is the island where a small group of people plan to enjoy two months of Summer rest and relaxation. The island is shaped like a crescent Moon, and is uninhabited by any animals.

Exploration

While the retired Reverend Timothy Maloney and his wife settle down for the evening, the three youngsters—Joan, their free-spirited daughter, family friend, Mr Hubbard, and Peter Sangree, a timid young Canadian, who is one of Timothy's adult students—go exploring.

At the far side of the small island, Joan wishes they had their canoe so they could visit some of the other islands, and although Hubbard offers to fetch it, she insists that Peter goes.

Unease

She explains that she feels uncomfortable alone in Peter's presence, as if uncertain what he might do. Hubbard understands the lad is infatuated with this beautiful, young woman and mentions this to her. She knows this already, of course, and describes her unease as a sort of fear that he might unleash something uncontrollable within her, something dark and powerful, the equal of something in him.

The following nights are haunted by a mysterious dog-like animal howling and scratching around the camp, trying to get at Joan. The party mounts a thorough search of the island, guns in hand, but the animal's trail does not leave the camp, and no trace of the animal is found.

Fascination with Wolves

Many people have tried to harness the powers of Nature, and in the Middle Ages, when belief in the supernatural was widespread—whether god, devils, or simply natural forces—magic and alchemy were widely explored. Many spell books, known as "grimoires," were devoted to black magic.

In *The Book of the Sacred Magic of Abra-Melin the Mage* by Abraham the Jew (1458, translated by S.L. MacGregor-Mathers in 1898), a long and complex magical ritual is described. This ceremony is designed to evoke the Holy Guardian Angel, after which the successful magician will gain mastery over the hierarchy of demons. Having controlled them, he is free to use them for holy purposes. One of these is to transform a man into a wolf (Book Three, Chapter IX).

This metamorphosis is simply achieved by writing the square on a piece of paper (see right), showing it the man, and then suddenly bringing it into contact with his body. The transformation will take place immediately. However, the grimoire cautions us that what the magician has actually achieved is merely a form of fascination or illusion—the man is not physically changed, but merely appears to be changed.

To return the wolf to human form, the magician places the square on the wolf's head and strikes it smartly with his wand.

While this might be a good party trick, like a hypnotist's power of suggestion making people behave oddly, it is difficult to see how it could be used to serve a sacred purpose.

Perhaps, by instilling new strength and confidence in somebody, it could enable them to achieve something worthwhile; or perhaps the transformed person might perform some useful role as a guardian to another, who is busy with holy works.

D	I	S	E	E	B	E	H
I	S	A	R	T	R	I	E
S	A	R	G	E	I	R	B
E	R	B	O	N	E	T	E
E	T	O	N	O	G	R	E
B	A	R	O	B	R	A	S
E	R	A	T	R	A	S	I
H	E	B	E	E	S	I	D

Creature emerges

When Hubbard holds a lone vigil he sees the creature emerge from Peter's tent, yet Peter is still sleeping within. Eventually the monster returns to Peter's tent and melts back into his body. The campers call on the help of paranormal researcher John Silence.

John proposes that the island is haunted by a werewolf. He explains that the soul of a truly wild place, the spirit of the wilderness can lure people away from their civilized nature and captivate them; they lose the trappings of social conformity, and revert to a primal, untamed state that mirrors their environment. If that person has a fractured personality, with their emotions divorced from their reason, then it may occur that their double breaks loose and walks free in an appropriate shape—in this case as a wolf.

Indian ancestry

John suspects Peter's ability to project his astral from his physical body is due to his partial Canadian Indian ancestry. He confides in Timothy and Hubbard that although the werewolf is a creation of the young man's love—pure and devout—it is unrestrained and in its fierce yearning for union it may inadvertently injure or even kill the object of its desire.

If, John declares, the astral body is prevented from returning to its physical host, then the man may never wake again, or if he does, he will be insane. And if the astral wolf is killed, the man too will die. Laying such a werewolf to rest is no simple matter.

Sleepwalking

That night, Timothy takes his gun and his Bible, and sets off to guard his daughter's tent. John and Hubbard watch as the werewolf creeps out of Peter's tent and into the moonlight. It howls piteously. But this time its howl is answered from the other wing of the island, from the direction of the women's tents. The two men follow the loping beast and arrive to see Joan standing out in the open. Her eyes are glazed—she is sleepwalking. She has come to meet her suitor, and she welcomes his approach.

Then a pistol shot cracks the night, and the wounded wolf leaps away into the shadow of the night. Simultaneously, a cry rises from Peter's tent, and John races back toward him. Hubbard comforts Joan, who has awakened full of yearning for her dream lover, and Timothy arrives thinking he has saved her from the beast.

Strange wounds

John arrives to find Peter delirious and feverish in his tent. He has two strange wounds that, impossibly, showed no signs of physical damage, as if they are superimposed on his body, not part of it. These strange marks that were caused when the bullet passed through his astral body would remain, John says, until just before Peter's death when the astral body leaves the physical body and takes its scars with it.

In the morning, Joan enters Peter's tent, and he instantly awakens now she has consciously recognized the love that she feels and has always felt for him. In this way the werewolf is, though

uncontrolled, the vehicle by which two lovers come together. This is an unusual werewolf love story because it ends happily.

FAIRYTALES THAT BITE

It is perhaps shocking that Little Red Riding Hood, the famous but also truly gruesome fairytale, is such a firm favorite in the nursery. After all, when the girl in the red cloak visits her grandmother in the wood she discovers a wolf has not only devoured the old lady, but now intends to eat her as well.

Appropriately told

Such a terrifying tale really doesn't seem appropriate for a toddler to hear in the dark of night. When we're on the brink of sleep, the thought of being eaten alive could easily nudge someone right over the edge into the scary world of nightmares.

But of course the secret is not what you say but the way that you say it. When the storyteller completes the long, slow pantomime build up "... And what big teeth you have," to which the wolf inevitably replies, "All the better to eat you with!" We all know how delightedly the wide-eyed child screams as Mom or Dad launches a "ferocious" attack—of tickles.

A GOOD SCARY MOMENT

It seems that even small children love a good scare, so long as everything comes out all right at the end. Even later, when we grow up, a really scary moment in a movie is a great excuse to cuddle up close to our boy- or girlfriend in the cozy dark of the cinema. This shudder of intimate pleasure is a gift the werewolf movie has always been happy to provide.

The origins of Little Red Riding Hood

But behind the fun and games lurks a deeper, and even darker truth. In this fairytale, the girl finds trouble at the end of her journey because she disobeyed a simple instruction.

The tale tells us that her mother warns her not to stray from the path and go into the woods. However, as she follows the forest track to her grandmother's house, a wolf approaches her and tries to tempt her away from the path.

Self-will

Her act of self-will in following the wolf away from the straight and narrow, to wander in the wild wood, informs us that Red is no longer a child. She has claimed her independence, which means she is free to make her own choices, and to make her own mistakes.

It is a delicate matter how the wolf seduces us. He seems to know all our weaknesses, and plays upon them expertly. Sometimes we may simply succumb to the lure of forbidden fruit. But mostly we give in because of our own instinctive knowledge that we must all, each of us, find our own individual path through life.

Levels of meaning

We can peel away the layers of the story of Little Red Riding Hood like onion skins, and find many levels of meaning. At its heart, the wolf is setting

us the challenge of whether or not we can handle the raw energy and excitement of being alive. Our animal instincts and desires—the wolf within us—can lead us badly astray.

There is no doubt that when we leave the well-trodden path we place ourselves in danger. And, yes, it can be fatal. Yet this story, which sees the wolf eat the child, has a twist in its tail. Some versions have an ending that reminds us not everything in the forest is after our blood. Just in the nick of time, a hunter who has been trailing the wolf, arrives and slits open the wolf's belly. From out of the body of the beast slips both granny and Red, whole as if reborn.

The rocks

What the girl does next seems extraordinary, though this varies from version to version: she grabs some rocks and stuffs them inside the wolf, which is still alive, and sews it up again. As the wounded creature tries to leap away toward the forest, the rocks prove to be too great a burden and the creature's heart breaks, killing it instantly. The rocks that bind the wolf to its doom are symbols of the weight of experience that the girl—a young woman now—has earned. She has learned grave lessons, but now she knows how to defeat the wolf and will never be caught again.

IVAN, THE FIREBIRD, AND THE WOLF

Of course, the wolf should not always be assumed to be guilty of murderous malevolence. He may have abilities that prove of invaluable assistance. There are many versions of this traditional Eastern European folk tale, which was recorded by Alexander Afnasev, the Russian equivalent of the Grimm brothers, in his vast collection, *Russian Folk Tales*.

A quest

In this tale, like both his elder brothers before him, Ivan rides out on a quest for the Firebird (which had stolen golden apples from his father) when a great gray wolf leaps up and snatches the horse from under him. Ivan is resolute in his quest and proceeds on foot, walking until weariness nearly claims his life. Then the gray wolf appears on the path before him.

Making amends

The wolf speaks, apologizing for eating his horse, and offers to make amends by being of service to Ivan. Ivan says he wishes to find the firebird. The wolf invites Ivan onto his back and runs off 20 times faster than a horse. Arriving at a vast stone wall, in the dark of the night, the wolf tells Ivan to climb over and there, in the garden, fetch the firebird out of its golden cage. Ivan climbs and finds the firebird, but in his stupid haste, he does not take it out of its cage, but tries to carry off the

WHAT BIG TEETH YOU HAVE...

In many old versions of *Little Red Riding Hood* (this illustration is from a German retelling), the girl is swallowed whole, but is soon delivered alive and well from the belly of the beast. Just like her, we may all be overtaken by events over which we have little control, and are fortunate to emerge intact.

firebird, cage and all. The cage is connected by invisible threads to all manner of instruments that set up an alarm, and Ivan is captured. The owner threatens to treat Ivan as a common thief, but relents and offers to give him the firebird in return for the horse with the golden mane, which he says is owed to him.

The quest

Empty-handed, Ivan returns to the gray wolf, weeping. The gray wolf tells him to climb on his back and, running 50 times faster than a horse, they soon arrive at the stables of the horse with the golden mane. The wolf tells Ivan to climb in and fetch the horse, and only the horse.

Capture

Ivan sneaks in and, in his haste, fetches not only the horse but its bridle, too, which again sets off loud alarms, and Ivan is captured. The owner threatens to treat Ivan as a common thief, but relents and offers to give him the horse with the golden mane in return for bringing him the princess he longs to wed—Helen the Beautiful.

Empty-handed, Ivan returns to the gray wolf, weeping. The gray wolf tells him to climb on his back and, running a hundred times faster than a horse, they arrive at the golden railings of the princess's garden. The wolf tells Ivan to stay and wait, which he does, resting under an oak tree.

Love at first sight

The wolf creeps into the garden and snatches away the princess. He carries her to Ivan, where they fall in love at first sight. Even with both Ivan and Helen on his back, the wolf easily outruns the soldiers, who try to pursue them. Arriving back at the stables of the horse with the golden mane, Ivan weeps at the prospect of losing his beloved Helen. The wolf thumps his paw on the damp soil and instantly turns into the exact double of the princess.

Leaving the real Helen in hiding, Ivan presents the wolf-princess to the owner of the horse with the golden mane, and receives his prize. Ivan rides away on the horse with the golden mane, collects the real Helen, and heads away to safety.

Transformation

After three days, shortly before the wedding, Ivan calls the gray wolf, who is out on the open steppe strolling with her ladies-in-waiting. Instantly the wolf transforms into his natural form and leaps away, running far too quickly for the ladies and soldiers to pursue. Soon he rejoins Ivan.

Arriving at the home of the firebird, Ivan asks the wolf to use trickery again, so he might keep the horse with the golden mane. Leaving Helen with the real horse with the golden mane in hiding, Ivan presents the wolf-horse to the owner of the firebird, and receives his prize.

Ivan walks away, collects Helen and the real horse, and heads away to safety. After three days, while the new owner is riding the wolf-horse on the open steppe, Ivan calls the gray wolf, who transforms into his natural form, and leaps away, running far too quickly for anyone to pursue. Soon he rejoins Ivan.

Debt paid

When they arrive at the place where the gray wolf snatched Ivan's horse, the wolf announces his debt paid in full and leaves. As chance would have it, that night, Ivan, Helen the Beautiful, the horse with the golden mane, and the firebird, are seen by Ivan's two elder brothers. Knowing their father will give half his kingdom to whoever returns with the firebird, the elder brothers conspire to steal it.

Casting lots

They kill Ivan, cutting his body into small pieces, and cast lots to see who gets the firebird, the horse, and Helen. They force Helen at knifepoint to agree to say they, not Ivan, had found the firebird, and return in triumph to their father, who duly gives half his kingdom to one son, and arranges the wedding for the other. Having followed the scent of slaughter, the gray wolf finds Ivan's body. A mother crow and two fledglings arrive to feast. The wolf snatches one of the young birds. The mother crow pleads with the wolf to let it go, and the wolf agrees on condition that she flies to a secret place that only birds can reach, where there are two springs of water, and she is to bring back a bottle of each.

Reforming

When the mother crow returns with the bottles, the wolf rends her chick apart. Then he takes the water of the spring of death and sprinkles some over the scattered pieces, which rapidly join back together. Then he sprinkles some water of the spring of life onto the reformed body; life returns to the young bird, which flies back to its mother.

Final farewell

The wolf repeats the process with Ivan, who awakes as if from a long sleep. The wolf carries him to his father's court, and there bids him a final farewell. Ivan enters, to the astonishment of all, and Helen tells the truth of the adventure. The elder sons are imprisoned and Ivan is given half his father's kingdom, and Helen's wedding is given to Ivan. They live in such joy and love that neither could bear to be apart from the other.

DIFFERENT FACETS

The people in a myth like Firebird can represent the different facets of a single person—the reader—making everyone who reads it a human–wolf combination—a werewolf!

We must each find our own truth reflected in this powerful story, but an obvious theme is the misuse of power. From the moment the wolf acts on instinct and devours the horse, he is morally bound to make amends.

Serving another

Changing from the self-serving tyrant he was, he comes to serve someone else. In the end, the wolf uses his destructive ability to put things right. By involving the birds, he gains control over an otherwise impossible situation, and achieves the magical resurrection of the hero—who had himself suffered at the hands of those who believed that "might is right."

Many times over, the hero learned that without such a strong, wise companion, he could never have succeeded in his quest to find love at last.

The Burning Times

European witches famously suffered during the Inquisition, but suspected werewolves were also vigorously persecuted and were frequently consigned to the flames.

WEREWOLVES MET THEIR DOOM

During the popular frenzy against lycanthropes, in 1541 the university town of Pavia in northern Italy had been under Spanish rule for just over 15 years, when a self-confessed werewolf met his doom. The peasant, as reported by Job Fincel in his book *de Mirabilibus*, believed himself to be a wolf, and had frequently submitted to his bestial cravings, attacking many men in open countryside and tearing them apart.

Inside the skin

When eventually captured, he insisted he was a wolf and gave a rather clever answer to the obvious question of his lack of a furry pelt: the hair grew, he said, on the inside of his skin. His captors seized upon this and cut deeply into his arms and legs, searching for the fur. Although no such hair was found, their victim, the murderous psychopath, died from his wounds.

THE CASE OF PETER STUBBE

Arguably the single most famous example of the horrors of lycanthropy answered by the brutality of medieval justice, is the case of Peter Stubbe (or Stump), who met his doom in 1590. His deeds and punishment were widely published at the time, with an account being printed in English (*A true discourse. Declaring the damnable life and death of one Stubbe Peeter, a most wicked sorcerer*, 1590). This pamphlet, which contained information produced, if not under actual torture then definitely under the threat of torture, and which may not therefore be completely reliable in matters of fact, tells the story presented at the trial. He was born in the village of Epprath, near Bedburg in the region of Cologne, Germany, and had already earnt a bad reputation by the time he was 12 years old.

A pact

He had, it is said, entered into a pact with the Devil, who promised him whatever his heart desired. Spurning wealth and position, he requested only that he could transform into the shape of a beast, and slake his appetite for killing men, women, and children.

A magic belt

The Devil granted his wish by giving Peter a magic girdle or belt (the sense of the original word "girdle" has changed since medieval times, so has become misleading).

As soon as Peter fastened the belt around his waist he became a ferocious wolf with a large body and great strength; his big eyes sparkled like a firebrand, and his wide mouth was filled with strong, sharp teeth. As soon as he took off the

belt, he instantly reverted to human form, with nothing to show that he had ever changed.

Attacking without mercy

Delighted, Peter stalked the fields, and even the streets, in the guise of the wolf, seeking anyone who had given him a sense of hurt. Finding his prey he would tear out their throats and rend their bodies limb from limb. He also attacked girls or young women working or playing in the fields, either alone or in groups, and chasing the one that most caught his fancy, he overpowered, ravished, and killed her without mercy.

In human form, he would walk the streets of the local villages and towns as if he were an ordinary

WOLF IN MAN'S CLOTHING

A spate of wolf attacks in the town of Anbach (Germany) occurred in 1685, soon after a hated mayor died, and people believed that he had risen from the grave as a werewolf. They finally caught and killed the animal when it jumped into a well. They dressed it to look like the mayor and hung it from a gibbet.

man; civil and polite. He would greet and converse with the bereaved parents and friends of his victims, and no one suspected his crimes.

Delight

In the space of a few years he slaughtered 13 children and two pregnant young women, whose babies were savagely torn from their wombs. He delighted in eating their hearts, still beating and hot, which he savored as a great delicacy.

He had sired a son and a daughter in the years before his werewolfism took root, but one day while Peter and the boy were out in the fields, he drew him aside into the woods. There, Peter snaked his wolf belt around himself and killed the youth. He cracked open his skull and ate the brains, relishing it as the most tender morsel.

Cravings

When his daughter Beell (Sybil) blossomed into womanhood, she was beautiful and of good grace, and Peter was drawn to her, fathering a child by his incestuous passion. He also seduced his sister and Katherine Trompin, a local woman.

THE STUFF OF NIGHTMARE 

This woodcut from the 1590 pamphlet shows the story of the rampaging werewolf, the villagers' pursuit of it, and the capture and trial of Peter Stubbe; then follows the grisly details of his execution, along with his daughter Beell and mistress Katherine Trompin.

The last strike

His killing, though, was destined to draw to a close, but not by his design. In wolf form he attacked a little group of children playing in a field of cows nursing calves, but providence provided that the girl he grabbed by the neck wore a stout collar that prevented his teeth sinking into her throat.

The alarm raised by the other children so affected the cows that their instinct to protect their calves made them stampede toward the wolf, driving him away and saving the girl.

Efforts rewarded

Having suffered attacks for 25 years, the local people were well prepared to launch a search party at short notice to hunt the wolf, and at last their efforts were rewarded.

With mastiff hounds they tracked and chased their quarry until they finally surrounded him. With nowhere left to run, the wolf ducked for cover, slid off his belt, and where wolf had been there now appeared Peter Stubbe—nonchalantly strolling along.

The hunters took him to the magistrates at Bedburg, who put him to the rack. Terrified at the prospect of prolonged torture, Peter confessed to these devilish crimes. The magic belt was not with him when he was captured, and despite a thorough search being made of the valley where he supposedly discarded it, no trace was ever found. The people supposed that the Devil had reclaimed his damnable treasure. The magistrates made diligent and painstaking enquiries, and soon arrived at the conviction that both his daughter, Beell, and Katherine Trompin were his accomplices.

Public execution

On 31 October 1589 Peter Stubbe was publicly executed before an audience that included peers and princes. First, he was stripped and bound to a large wheel on the ground. A pair of large, two-handed pincers were placed in a brazier beside him until the metal burned red hot; this instrument was then applied to his body so that it tore away a chunk of flesh from the bone. Not once, or twice, was this procedure carried out, but ten times.

A blunt axe, with its head made of heavy wood, was used time and again to smash the bones in his arms and legs. Only then was he killed by decapitation. His lifeless body was dragged from the wheel and tied to the nearby stake standing in the midst of a large heap of firewood. Rising from this vast unlit pyre were two further stakes, and

WEREWOLF VERSUS DOGS

Bishop Olaus Magnus wrote of a wealthy lady of Livonia, Latvia, who did not believe in werewolves. Her servant went into a cellar and changed himself into one. When he emerged as a wolf, the lady's dogs gouged out an eye and chased him away. The servant returned the next day, with only one eye.

bound to these unyielding poles were the two women waiting for their lives to be consumed by the flames kindled below.

A darker motive
Those who witnessed the end of this unholy trinity would not have forgotten the sight, the sounds, and the smells of the scene. This was the intention, of course; to dissuade anyone from behaving in the same way. But modern historians see a darker motive for the unusual severity with which these three were treated.

Peter Stubbe had been a successful farmer whose wealth and bearing exerted considerable local influence in the community. But these were troubled times, and when the Lord of Bedburg declared his allegiance to Protestantism, it is more than probable that Peter followed suit.

Engineered trial
The declaration of this wide-scale religious conversion brought war to the region, with soldiers and mercenaries bringing a tide of death to the towns and villages so that violence and murder became commonplace.

The fighting came to an end in 1587 with the victory of the Roman Catholic army, and a new lord ruled in Bedburg castle. Fired with religious conviction to punish the heretics, and bolstered by hired killers who pacified resistance, the Catholic lord may well have engineered the trial to provide an unforgettable example to all, as a shocking demonstration of how dissent would be dealt with.

THE BEAST IN MAN

The 17th-century artist Charles le Brun was fascinated by mankind's obvious similarity to other members of the animal kingdom. In this engraving, simply entitled "Werewolf," he shows how closely man resembles the wolf.

Whether Peter Stubbe was a serial killer with a lycanthropic psychosis, and his daughter Beell and lover Katherine were accomplices deserving of capital punishment, we may never know. But their awful story will continue to be told in hushed voices when the werewolf and the burning times are brought to mind.

THE JURGENSBERG TRIAL

One of the most famous lycanthropy trials took place in 1692 at Jürgensberg, Livonia (an area contained by modern Estonia and Latvia). An 80-year-old man was accused of having made a pact with the Devil, a charge he strongly denied, although he did admit to being a werewolf.

Across the sea
He said that three nights each year, on the Christian feasts of Pentecost, St John, and St Lucy, he and all the other "hounds of God" would sally forth across the sea to do battle with the mustered witches and their commander, the Devil. If he and his fellow crusading werewolves were unsuccessful in defeating the forces of evil, the

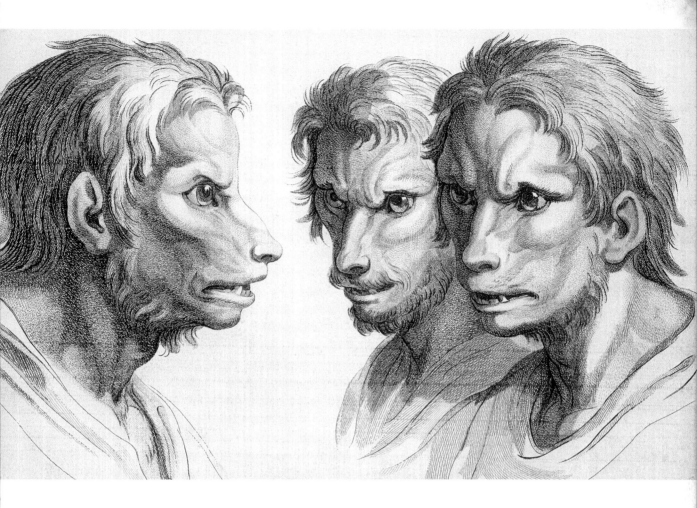

witches would bring famine to the community. The werewolves protected the crops and ensured the survival of the harvest. While he remained confident he would receive his due reward in Paradise, the authorities gave him ten lashes of the whip.

MIRROR IMAGE

When we see the natural intelligence in a wolf's eyes, watch how they work together, live together and communicate, we feel we're meeting a mind like our own. This is not surprising, as we are both highly evolved mammals. Our old mistake was to assume an evil man inhabited the wolf's body. When we recognize the animal as being innately part human, our fear can fade, and we can accept it, instead, as a kind of "wolfwere."

Chapter 5

Defence Against the Werewolf

Fangs or Furry?

Werewolves can be kindly creatures whose greatest wish is for everyone to get on with each other. As such, they surely have the natural right to public tolerance, even if they don't receive positive support for their lifestyle. But other werewolves are cast in a different mold—with more emphasis on fangs than furriness—and these cause more than their fair share of mischief.

The strongest weapon

If you don't have any of the physical remedies mentioned in this chapter, love is probably your strongest weapon. As most poignantly portrayed in *An American Werewolf in London* (see page 77), some werewolves may only be killed when they desire death.

Love inspires the werewolf to undertake the ultimate self-sacrifice, dying to protect the one they love, from themselves. Exercising self-control after transformation is usually impossible, but while the transformation is still under way, the human strength of will can sometimes suppress the rising rage and calm the werewolves down.

Pacification

One way of achieving this pacification is to think of ordinary, mundane things. In *Kitty and the Midnight Hour* (see page 107) the heroine has an orderly list of word associations that start from cold water and ice, range through broccoli and Brussels sprouts, to green, light, peace, and music, and culminate in the aria "Sheep May Safely Graze" (by Johann Sebastian Bach).

Running water

A persistent legend suggests the best thing to do if you're being pursued by a werewolf is to jump in a river, or even a stream; the idea being that a werewolf reverts to human form when bathed in running water. This ancient idea is echoed in the TV drama *Being Human* (see pages 86–7), where the reluctant werewolf uses streams as boundaries to stop himself roaming far.

Silver salvation

A silver bullet is by far the best-known way to kill a werewolf, and the high-tech silver nitrate bullet used against the Lycan in *Underworld* (see pages 57–9) is the 21st-century successor to this traditional method. The silver bullet is not ancient, as firearms are a relatively recent invention, and neither were they exclusively aimed at werewolves—they were the hunter's weapon of choice against witches who had transformed into any creature.

The bullet used in *Blood and Chocolate* (see page 111) was made from a silver pentagram pendant, combining both the power of the pentagram (as seen in *The Wolf Man*) and the metal of choice. Although its metal is not specified, the gypsy pendant of protection against the curse of the werewolf in *The Wolf Man* (see page 72) certainly

looks like silver. The use of the silver piercing ring in *Ginger Snaps* (see page 100), the silver head on the walking stick in *The Wolf Man*, and the silver letter opener in *Dog Soldiers* (see page 68) are other innovative uses of silver. Silver has long been associated with the Moon (while gold corresponds to the Sun), so its use as a weapon under the shining, full Moon is poetically just. Because silver belongs to the same supernatural realm as the lunar lycanthrope, it can be effective against him. Ordinary metals have no power to exist in that impossible creature's world, and so cannot hurt the werewolf.

THE WEREWOLF THAT WASN'T

Despite this emotive image making many appearances in the publicity for *The Curse of the Werewolf* (1961), it doesn't appear in the movie. It actually shows the adult Leon (Oliver Reed) in his werewolf form, carrying his mother (Yvonne Romain), who is supposed to have died just after he was born.

Wolfsbane

This plant has a long association with werewolves, and is well-known for its poisonous properties. Wolfsbane *(Aconitum vulparia)* is one of more than several hundred species and sub-species in the aconite plant family, of which most grow in mountainous regions of the Northern Hemisphere; the natural habitat of the wolf.

Poison devoured

Its name indicates its power against wolves as a bane or deadly poison. When mixed with bait and devoured by a wolf, or even daubed on arrowheads fired into the animal's body, the toxins can prove fatal.

The aconite plant family includes northern wolfsbane (*Aconitum lycoctonum*) and monkshood (*Aconitum napellus*). Because wolfsbane and monkshood are closely related and each contains powerful toxins, their significance in folklore has become muddled, allowing a fusing of ideas. This has happened despite the very clear visual distinction of wolfsbane's flowers being yellow, while monkshood flowers are a dark, purplish blue. For example, in *Ginger Snaps* (see page 100), a simple solution of dried monkshood can inhibit the transition from human to wolf, or even reverse it.

Wolfsbane in fiction

Wolfsbane is generally regarded as a werewolf repellent, protecting people from the beast, and eating, or even smelling it, can make a werewolf run away or even die. In *Kitty and the Midnight Hour* (see pages 107–8), the newly created werewolf, Kitty, tried to free herself from the curse and drank some wolfsbane tea on the night of the new Moon, but it didn't work and made her sick.

On the other hand, the iconic movie *The Wolf Man* (see page 71) specifically mentions bright moonlight and flowering wolfsbane as the two conditions under which the transformation from man to werewolf may be made.

Poisonous plants

Aconite was an ingredient in some so-called witches' ointments that supposedly enabled a witch to fly and perhaps shape-shift. It could certainly provide a tingling sensation on the skin, followed by numbness, and it could also produce hallucinations, but as the quantity needed for this would be close to a fatal dose, it is unlikely to have been used regularly for this purpose.

The folklore is confused about the magical properties of these plants, and that could be because a large proportion of people who investigated them probably died in the attempt. Wolfsbane and monkshood are poisonous to humans, and under no circumstances should any part of the plants be eaten; even touching them can cause severe reactions and should be avoided at all costs.

I. Aconitum Lycocto, num flore Delphinij.

II. Aconitum Lycoctonum flore luteo.

BEAUTIFUL BUT DEADLY

Wolfsbane blooms in a variety of colors, but their exotic-looking flowers all share the same sinister reputation, as these plants contain a lethal poison. These illustrations of *Aconitum lycoctonum,* are from the book of botanical specimens by Basilius Besler (*Hortus Eystettensis*, 1613).

A Wolf in the Home?

A dog is three meals away from being a wolf; so says a common proverb commenting on the fact that the family pet still has the instincts of its genetic forebear, the wolf. The Latin name for the dog is *Canis lupus familiaris,* which shows its pedigree: *Canis lupus* is the wild Gray Wolf, also known as the Timber Wolf.

FORMING A PACK

It takes as few as two dogs to form a pack and, in stressful situations, they can spontaneously break away from human control and start to play by their own rules. In those respects, dogs are similar to people who lose self-control in difficult circumstances and do things in a gang that they would never dream of doing alone.

DANGER OF DOGS

It is the very rare exception that proves the rule, but dog attacks do happen. Most bite victims that make the headlines are babies and young children, and the main reason for this (apart from being particularly tragic) is that while adults can take a bite or two and survive, young children are much smaller and more vulnerable.

Toddlers and dogs

The best advice is never to leave a young child unattended with a dog. This is because all toddlers have infinite curiosity and will explore everything—poking, prodding, twisting, and pinching everything in their path. Dogs will, naturally, feel that this treatment is unfair. A quiet growl would alert an adult to a dog's feelings, but a young child will not recognize that as a threat and may even repeat their actions just to hear the sound again.

Domesticated wolves?

Some people even think about having a wolf as a pet. Wolves can look awfully cute as cubs, but they inevitably grow into wild animals. There are many differences between a wolf and a dog, not least of which is the fact that a wolf's instinct is to climb to the top of the pack hierarchy. A wolf will keep testing human dominance and never give up trying to defeat us.

Competition for the dominance of a pack has only been observed to lead to the death of an alpha when the animals are in captivity, for example in a zoo. Normal wolf behavior would be to accept defeat and walk away from the fight. Captive wolves, including those raised in a domestic environment, can live for 15 years, making the relationship between owner and wolf a long, hard struggle, and few people can successfully meet the commitment.

Bad guard dogs

Despite the common tradition of the werewolf being used to guard the vampire's lair, wolves actually make very bad guard dogs. Although they may detect an intruder much earlier than any of us, either by scent or hearing, the wolf is likely just to give a single, warning bark, and do nothing more. He will consider his duty done once he has alerted you to the fact that the intruder exists. Because we humans are the pack alpha, the wolf will expect us to lead the attack, and will wait for our signal before it does anything.

Adapted to freedom

Wolves are not wild dogs that we can domesticate; they are wild animals supremely adapted to living in complete freedom. Dogs certainly originated as wolves, and dogs of a suitable size can even still breed with wolves, creating wolfdogs. But dogs have the benefit of thousands of generations of domestication and selective breeding to help them fit in to the human lifestyle.

Almost all wolves in captivity feel utterly alienated, and this anxiety breeds aggression, making everyone's lives miserable and reinforcing the persistent misconception that wolves are evil.

Living the dream

There are many groups devoted to the wellbeing of wolves in the wild. Some focus on single issues such as reintroducing wolves to local habitats in which they were hunted to extinction. Others look at the overall global situation, and coordinate activities with other conservation groups. All need support.

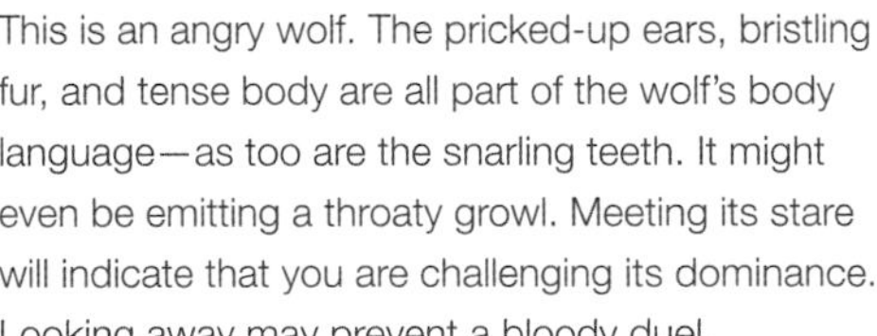

BE AFRAID...BE VERY AFRAID

This is an angry wolf. The pricked-up ears, bristling fur, and tense body are all part of the wolf's body language—as too are the snarling teeth. It might even be emitting a throaty growl. Meeting its stare will indicate that you are challenging its dominance. Looking away may prevent a bloody duel.

Harry Potter Tips

The *Harry Potter* stories contain many practical tips for overcoming common problems and one of the greatest of these pieces of advice is the Riddikulus Charm taught to the children by the werewolf Professor Lupin. Explained in *Harry Potter and the Prison of Azkaban*, this charm is fiendishly simple: it uses laughter to defeat an enemy that is using fear as its primary weapon.

Transformation

In the classroom the foe is a Boggart, which makes itself appear in the form of whatever scares its victim most. For Professor Lupin, this frightening form was the full Moon appearing in the night sky—the accursed sight that triggers his transformation into a ravenous wolf.

"Riddikulus"

Despite this appalling sight, the Professor musters his strength of mind and retaliates with the single word "Riddikulus" (pointing a magic wand is necessary for beginners, but an optional extra for advanced users). This charm forces the Boggart to lose its frightening shape, and become instead the shape of your own ridiculous, or laughable idea.

What happens next to Professor Lupin depends on whether you're reading the book or watching the movie. In the book, the Moon falls to the ground as a cockroach, which is demeaning but not really very funny; but in the movie the orb turns into the white face of a clown painted on a balloon, which suddenly has its nozzle opened, and it goes whizzing around the room, much to the delight of the children.

Visual impact

The book gives more examples of fears and their antidotes than the movie, but the sheer visual impact of the movie makes the charm very memorable. Working out our own versions to combat our own fears can be a very rewarding and powerful process.

The Homorphus Charm

The Harry Potter mythos contains one ray of hope for werewolves: the Homorphus Charm. This is said to be able to transform a werewolf from its wolf form back into human form. As such, it is effectively a cure when administered in monthly doses. Unfortunately, the charm is only mentioned by Professor Gilderoy Lockhart, an inveterate liar.

FACING FEAR

The saying "there is nothing to fear but fear itself" indicates the strength of the mental and physical paralysis that fear can cause. Werewolf professor Remus Lupin (David Thewlis) in *Harry Potter and the Prison of Azkaban* teaches his students to free themselves from fear and learn to fight effectively.

The Discovery of Lupinone

In 1992 a group of researchers from the Orphan Drug Research Institute (W.M. Davis PhD/H.G. Wellwuff MD PhD; Lou Garew MD; O.U. Kydd PhD) published their findings in an article entitled "Psychopharmacology of lycanthropy."

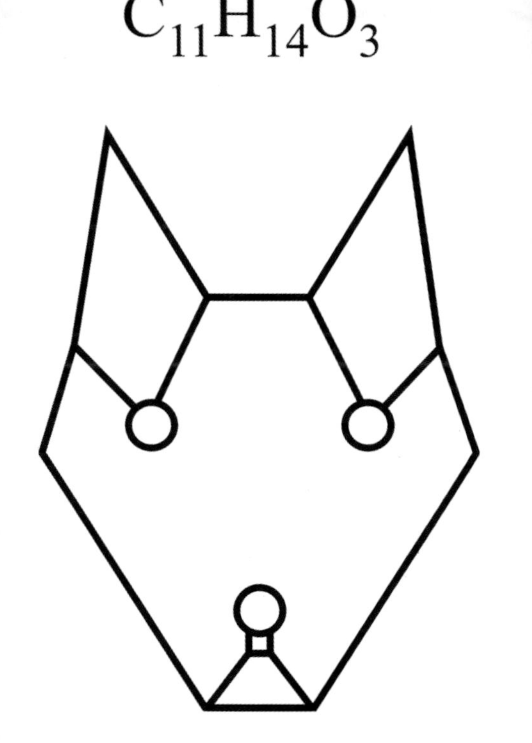

WEREWOLFISM IN FOLKLORE

The group conducted detailed studies of descendants of Native American people known commonly as Ruficolla, particularly from North Carolina and Minnesota in the USA. This tribe was selected for the persistence of werewolfism in its folklore and traditional rituals. And the results were extraordinary.

MOLECULAR MARKER

By collecting blood samples throughout the month, the team found a molecular marker whose quantity peaked regularly in time with the full Moon. They analyzed its chemical composition and determined its formula as C_{11} H_{14} O_3 (the same as the fragrance hyacinth acetal), and they named it lupinone.

By conducting low-dosage tests on gregarious laboratory lemmings, the team noted an increase in irritability and loss of social cohesion; but using a high dose on just one animal in the test group, they saw the untreated animals run away from the treated lemming.

MASK OF THE WOLF

This is the startling molecular model of the lycanthropogen—Lupinone—which is deemed responsible for the condition werewolfism. With a total of 28 atoms in the molecule, some researchers are looking for a possible link with the number of days between lunar cycles.

This latter effect they attribute to lupinone stimulating production of a non-sexual pheromone, a fearomone, that induces mass psychosis and panic in those nearby. The researchers hope to use these findings to develop a cure for human panic disorder.

LYCOMANIA IN HUMANS

Following tests of 615 human guinea pigs, they discovered lupinone by itself creates lycomania in people. However, when lupinone is coupled with lycanthrokinin, a peptide secreted by the pineal gland in the brain, while the test subject is in the presence of strong moonlight, a full lycanthropic transformation can be induced in an otherwise normal person.

Another practical application of the team's groundbreaking research involves discovery of lycanthrokinin receptors at the base of hair follicles. This promises rapid advances in commercial applications relating to the rapid hair growth associated with werewolf transformations.

TACKLING ALCOHOLISM

The team also hopes their research will help to tackle the perennial social problem of alcoholism. Preliminary results indicate that alcohol stimulates the body's production of lycanthropogens, which in turn elevates lycanthrokinin levels, and possibly triggers a full-blown lycanthropic episode. This could account for the primitive or even beastly behavior, accompanied by memory loss, that is frequently reported by binge drinkers.

By understanding the physiological source of lycanthropy we should at last be able to stop the superstitious fear and stigma attached to lycanthropes, and eventually offer a cure. Of course, there is every likelihood that this medical breakthrough will result first and foremost in the development of a new class of recreational drugs that will require stringent legislation to control.

Further study of the chemical constituents of lupinone (carbon, hydrogen, oxygen—CHO) suggests a possible link with Cho—a system of Tibetan Buddhism that explores transcendent knowledge through contemplation. These powerful techniques may calm the unbridled passions that accompany the wolf phase and help the werewolf cut the bonds that doom him to suffer.

The original article was published in the Canadian Medical Association Journal Vol 146, April 1st (or April Fool's Day). The full text of this incredible piece of research is currently available online.

Know Your Enemy

While we can discover much about werewolves from reading about them, we may discover more by spending time in a role-playing game (RPG). In the early 1990s, *Werewolf: the Apocalypse,* the second *World of Darkness* role-playing game, made its appearance. It is a variety of storytelling—indeed, the gamesmaster is called the Storyteller. RPGs involve a gathering of like-minded people who assume the personalities of characters in the game to act out scenarios determined by the Storyteller. RPGs demands interaction and cooperation to be successful.

In the game, the players take on the characters of different types of werewolves, who refer to themselves collectively as Garou. The main premise of the game is that the Garou were created to defend Gaia (the Earth) and her Umbra (the spirit world), which was born of the Wyld (the chaotic forces of nature). Two other forces exist: the Weaver, which creates structure and order, and the Wyrm, the destroyer. In the game, in its fruitless attempts to impose order on the Wyld, the Weaver has become insane and taken control of the Wyrm, driving it mad as well, and now the two forces threaten to tear the world apart. Creation is no longer in balance.

Protecting the Earth

The beauty of the game is that it allows the players to take on the characteristics of their chosen werewolf breed, tribe, and auspice and explore life as that creature. The overarching concept—protecting the Earth—teaches valuable lessons about ecology, while the interactions between the players provide learning experiences in tolerance and cooperation.

The Garou

The Garou are physically powerful and deeply spiritual beings who can shape-shift at will. Their abilities are inherited rather than acquired. They battle the forces of the Wyrm in an attempt to restore the balance of Nature. There are three breeds of Garou:

- ***Homid*** *Raised in human cultures, they know nothing of their heritage until their first Change. They are knowledgeable about the human world and at home with technology, but often have difficulty dealing with the wild side of their nature and the natural world.*
- ***Metis*** *The deformed and sterile offspring of two Garou. They are skilled warriors, and have an understanding of both the wild and human worlds.*
- ***Lupus*** *Born of wolves and with a primal and instinctive connection to Gaia (or the Earth). They have no understanding of human society and often blame humans for everything wrong in the world.*

Werewolf—the Party Game

Werewolf is an exciting and often noisy game of suspense and role play. This version by Andrew Plotkin works best with an odd number of players from seven to 17 in number.

Using shuffled pieces of paper, allocate each person a role: there will be one Narrator, one Village Psychic, two Werewolves, and all the remainder will be Villagers.

The Narrator reveals his/her identity, but everyone else has to keep theirs secret.

The Narrator declares it is night, and instructs everyone to close their eyes and bow their heads in sleep. The werewolves are invited to wake up and choose a victim (even using sign language, this can make give-away noises, so the Narrator may instruct everyone to hum, tap their fingers, feet, or whatever else makes some noise, to give the werewolves an advantage).

The Narrator instructs the werewolves to close their eyes and bow their heads in sleep after their feast. The Narrator invites the Village Psychic to see a vision in a dream, a vision that will truly reveal whether someone is a werewolf or not. The Village Psychic opens their eyes and silently points to someone, the Narrator gives them the thumbs up sign if that person is a werewolf, and the thumbs down if they are an ordinary Villager. Having learned a valuable truth, the Village Psychic goes back to sleep.

The Narrator declares it is day, invites everyone to open their eyes, and points out the person killed by the werewolves (preferably with a suitably gory description)! As soon as somebody is pronounced dead, they immediately show their identity on their piece of paper, and take no further part.

Everyone (except the Narrator) discusses who among them is innocent and who is a werewolf. They select their suspect by simple majority vote (the Narrator does not vote), and lynch them. That person is now dead.

The day is over, and tension mounts as night falls, and the remaining werewolf or werewolves select another victim.

Play continues until either both werewolves are lynched, or there is an equal number of Villagers and Werewolves—at which point the surviving werewolf (or werewolves) instantly attacks the remaining Villager (or Villagers) in a final frenzied feast.

Guiding Star

The pentagram, or five-pointed star, is associated with the werewolf in many ways.

THE STARRY HEAVENS

Firstly, it reminds us of the starry Heavens. Cruelly cold, these silvery lights gaze down upon the doomed werewolf that forever treads through the darkness. It is a bleak emblem of the curse itself. Yet it is also a talisman offering a prospect of hope and protection.

The pattern of four lower points surmounted by a fifth, is strongly reminiscent of our own body (four limbs and the head), and is often regarded as a sacred symbol of the human being.

The Greek philosopher Pythagoras (6th century BCE), saw the pentagram as a symbol that represented holistic health.

He saw the upper point, the head, as representing spirit, and the four lower points as the four sorts of matter: fire, water, air, and earth. Pythagoras and his followers believed these five elements made everything in the world—including us—proving the unity between us and our environment.

INTERCONNECTEDNESS

The pentagram stresses the interconnectedness of all aspects of life. Wiccans, modern white witches who widely use the pentagram in their rites, advocate balanced integration as essential to personal wellbeing. The challenge for the werewolf is to find a balance between the competing sides of their lives. In particular their great physical strength needs to be channeled into constructive ventures.

The human/wolf split is like a divorce between mind and body. The pentagram teaches us that the head is intimately connected with, and supported by, the body. It does not dominate it like a tyrant does.

Sexual themes are to be found throughout werewolf lore. But even the simple physical urges of the human animal are enough to supply not only big problems for the werewolf, but a remarkable last link with the pentagram.

ASTRONOMICAL COINCIDENCE

In the third millennium BCE the Mesopotamian civilization of Akkad discovered a unique astronomical coincidence that makes the planet Venus appear to complete her orbital cycle five times every eight years. The planet's cycle can be plotted on the encircling Zodiac, and if a line is drawn from any point to its recurrence 584

DECIPHERING A SACRED SYMBOL 

Venus orbits the golden Sun, marking five points on the encircling zodiac. This circle, the symbol of spirit, is placed above the equal-armed cross that signifies matter. Together, circle and cross form the traditional symbol of Venus. Her color is the green of the fertile Earth, outlined against the black sky.

days later, and so on... It will draw a pentagram. This distinctive celestial pattern became enshrined in the iconography of their goddess of the planet—Ishtar—goddess of love, sex, and war. Our own name for this planet—Venus—reinforces its link with the goddess of physical love.

INTEGRATION

The pentagram shows the werewolf the wisdom of integrating his or her urges in a creative way. In particular, the Wiccan celebration of sexuality liberated from the concept of sin, and raised to the level of a holy sacrament, offers the prospect of complete, ultimate unification.

Glossary

Alpha male/female The dominant animal in a pack.

Anthropology The study of different cultures, beliefs, and societies around the world.

Anthropomorphic With human characteristics: for example an animal in a story who speaks and wears clothes.

Astral body The part of a person that can move outside of the body; a kind of psychic projection.

Astral plane One place where an astral body can visit. It is not a physical place, but is thought to be somewhere between the physical world and the Heavens. The term is not specific to any one religion and many faiths have a concept of something that could be interpreted as an astral plane.

Auspice A sign that indicates future events, like an omen.

B-Movie A low-budget movie that often has acquired cult status. The name originates from the double features that used to be shown at cinemas. The A-Movie would be the head-lining feature, while the B-Movie would be something less well known.

Baneful Harmful, deadly, or sinister.

Berserkers Ancient Norse warriors, who wore animal skins and called on the animals' powers in battle. The phrase "to go berserk" comes from their impressive and deadly fighting skills.

Bestial Animal-like, depraved. Either with animal-like habits, violence, or sub-human intelligence.

Bipedal On two legs.

Blasphemy An act that demonstrates disrespect for God or something held sacred. It could be something spoken, written, or acted out.

Chivalry Knightly. The chivalrous ideal, first developed in medieval times, relates to being brave, honorable, courteous, and respectful toward women.

Conjure To bring something about, almost magically. Someone could conjure up a spirit or a storm, or appear to conjure with a card trick. Stories and music conjure images in our minds.

Corporeal Physical and actually in existence. Something non-corporeal could be a ghost or spirit.

Cryptid An unidentified animal or creature secret to zoology (*see* Cryptozoology.)

Cryptozoology The study of obscure or "hidden" creatures ("cryptids"), such as the Loch Ness Monster or the big cats of Britain.

Death Dealers A band of elite vampire warriors in the *Underworld* movie series, dedicated to exterminating all Lycans.

Deity A god or goddess. It can also describe the holiness of a god.

Diabolical Associated with the Devil. This could either mean something that has come from the Devil himself, or something so evil that is seems "devilish."

Ectoplasm The substance that spirits or ghostly figures are made from. It is non-corporeal, non-physical, and often transparent. Mediums in trances supposedly emit ectoplasm.

Eldritch Supernatural, weird, or unearthly. Something not explainable by normal reasoning.

Enchantress A female who is either so attractive or charming (enchanting) that she seems to "cast a spell" on people; or a woman who actually practices magic.

Excommunication When someone is formally banned from places of worship. Though not necessarily a permanent ban, this is seen to reduce a person's chances significantly of getting to Heaven, and also means the person cannot be buried in consecrated (blessed) ground.

Exhumation The digging up and removing of a body from its grave.

Fey Otherworldly, magical. Can also indicate an ability to see the future. The word suggests a certain degree of femininity, as well.

Firebird A magical, glowing bird from Russian folklore. The term is also used to describe a variety of birds with firey-colored feathers.

Genus A biological term for a "family" in plant or animal species. For example foxes, wolves, and dogs all come from the same genus.

Hallucinogenic Something that makes people hallucinate and see things that are not there. Illnesses, such as a fever, and some types of drugs can produce this effect.

Hybrid A cross between two species. For example, a mule is half horse and half donkey. A half-werewolf, half-vampire creature is formed either by being bitten by both (as in *Underworld*) or by having one werewolf parent and one vampire parent (as in *The Monster Club*).

Hypertrichosis A medical condition where a person produces too much body hair.

Lore Traditional tales, beliefs, and facts gathered on one subject or from one tradition. The word indicates that the knowledge is not proven fact, but more a collection of anecdotes, for example on how werewolves behave.

Loups-garoux Werewolves (French).

Lupine From the Latin *lupus*, meaning wolf-like.

Lycan Race of werewolves in the *Underworld* series of movies.

Lycanthrope Man or woman who is (or believes themselves to be) part wolf.

Lynching Putting somebody to death for something they have done, without a trial. It indicates that a group of people were involved in the killing.

Masquerade A costume party at which masks are worn. It can also mean a disguise or a deceptive pretence.

Monkshood Like wolfsbane, an *aconitum* species plant especially associated with werewolves.

Navajo Native American tribe from the south-west of the United States.

Occult Hidden or obscure, relating to the supernatural or beyond the knowledge of most humans. It also suggests something relating to magic or dark forces.

Pantomime A pantomime play is an anarchic, comedic, family-friendly play put on in Britain and Ireland, usually around Christmas-time. The plots are based around a fairytales, costumes are exaggerated, and the audience is encouraged to shout out.

Patronize To pay regularly for or to sponsor. A patron is a wealthy person who financially supports someone such as a favored artist. Some royal courts patronized people such as jesters or people prized for their "oddness," such as those with visually striking conditions.

Pelt Animal skin. It usually indicates that the fur is still on the skin.

Pentagram A five-pointed star often associated with witchcraft and the occult.

Persecution The ill-treatment of a person or group because of a particular characteristic or belief.

Phosphorescent Emitting light, something that glows in the dark. Some types of plants and animals glow in the dark.

Predator An animal which lives off other animals, hunting and killing them. It also suggests a certain amount of enjoyment of the chase and the kill.

Progeny Children or offspring. The term progeny can be localized (you and your siblings are your parents' progeny) or it can mean all those descended from one source many hundreds of years ago.

Rabid A person or animal suffering from the disease rabies. The disease eventually makes sufferers insane and prone to attacking others.

Romance A particular type of story common in medieval Europe, often dealing with quests, magic, and courtly love.

Ruficolla Gotcha! April Fool! (Whatever day it is that you're reading this.) This article was actually published in a real medical journal, but as an April Fool's prank.

Shaman A person from a tribal society who works as a go-between from the physical world to the spirit world. These people are often religious leaders or healers, and often use magic and prophecy to see and affect the future.

Skinwalker An evil Navajo witch that can shape-shift into various animals and often has superhuman strength or speed and telepathy.

Therianthrope A shape-shifter, part man, part beast.

Totem A symbolic animal or image. A respected emblem.

Transcendental Something supernatural or mystical. Something beyond common thought or understanding.

Transvection Another term for metamorphosis; used in *Werewolf of London.*

Unconsecrated Consecrated ground is ground that has been blessed for ritual purpose. Most often used to describe a burial ground such as a churchyard. Burial in unconsecrated ground was considered a punishment for the unchristened, suicides, witches, and those considered to have led evil lives.

Underworld A series of movies in which vampires and werewolves are at war, unbeknownst to humans. It moves from a contemporary urban setting to the two species' previous battles across the centuries.

Vulpine Fox-like. The term is also used to describe cunning and craftiness, as these are seen as fox-like characteristics.

Waning Decreasing. Usually used to describe the phase of the Moon when it is reducing in size after a full Moon.

Waxing Increasing. Usually used to describe the phase of the Moon when it is becoming full.

Wolfsbane The poisonous plant especially associated with werewolves.

Bibliography

Abraham the Jew, (trans. MacGregor-Mathers, S.L.) *The Book of the Sacred Magic of Abra-Melin the Mage*, London, Thorsons, 1976
Aesop (trans. Temple, Olivia) *The Complete Fables*, London, Penguin Classics, 2003
Anonymous, *A. True Discourse: Declaring the Damnable Life and Death of One Stubbe Peeter, a Most Wicked Sorcerer*, London, E Venge, 1590
Apollodorus (trans. Hard, Robin) *The Library of Greek Mythology*, Oxford, Oxford University Press, 1997
Beagle, Peter "Lila the Werewolf," in Pronzini, Bill (ed.), *Werewolf! A Chrestomathy of Lycanthropy*, New York, Arbor House, 1979
Bierce, Ambrose *The Devil's Dictionary*, New York, Dover Publications, 1958
Blackwood, Algernon *The Insanity of Jones and Other Tales*, London, Penguin, 1966
Brander, Gary *The Howling*, London, Arrow Books, 1978
Bremmer, Jan N. and Veenstra, Jan R. (eds.), *The Metamorphosis of Magic from Late Antiquity to the Early Modern Period*, Leuven (Belgium), Peeters Publishers, 2002
Bruce, Christopher W. *The Arthurian Name Dictionary*, Oxford, Taylor & Francis, 1999
Byron, Lord, *Don Juan*, Halifax, Milner and Sowerby, 1873
Carter, Angela *The Bloody Chamber*, London, Penguin, 1981.
Chetwynd-Hayes, R. *The Monster Club*, London, New English Library, 1976
Davis, W.M. and Wellwuff, H.G. and Garew, L. and Kydd, O.U. "Psychopharmacology of lycanthropy," *Canadian Medical Association Journal*, Volume 146, Issue 7, 1191–1197, 1992
Defonseca, Misha *Surviving with Wolves*, London, Piatkus, 2006
Dennis, Andrew, Foote, Peter, and Perkins, Richard (trans.) *Laws of Early Iceland: Gragas I : The Codex Regius of Gragas With Materials from Other Manuscripts*, Winnipeg, University of Manitoba Press, 1980
Fortune, Dion *Psychic Self-Defense*, York Beach, Red Wheel/Weiser, 2001
Gerald of Wales (trans. Seward, William Wenman) *Topographia Hibernica: Or the Topography of Ireland, Ancient and Modern*, Whitefish, Kessinger Publishing, 2008
Homer (trans. Rieu, E.) *The Odyssey*, London, Penguin Classics, 2003
Kramer, Heinrich and Sprenger, James (trans. Summers, Montague) *Malleus Maleficarum*, London, Arrow Books, 1971
Leadbeater, C.W. *The Astral Plane: Its Scenery, Inhabitants and Phenomena*, New York, Cosimo, 2005
Livy (trans. De Selincourt, Aubrey) *The Early History of Rome*: Books 1–5, London, Penguin Classics, 2005
Magnússon, Eiríkr *Völsunga Saga: The Story of the Volsungs and Niblungs*, Charleston, BiblioBazaar, 2008
Mallory, Sir Thomas (ed. Rhys, Sir John) *Sir Thomas Mallory Le Morte D'Arthur* Volume Two, London, Dent, 1956
Marie of France (trans. Burgess, Glyn) *The Lais of Marie de France: With Two Further Lais in the Original Old French*, London (UK), Penguin Classics, 2003
Marryat, Frederick *The Phantom Ship*, London, New English Library, 1975
Milne, F.A. (trans.) "Arthur and Gorlagon," *Folklore*, Vol. 15, No. 1, 40–67, 1904
O'Donnell, Elliott *Werwolves*, London, Methuen, 1912
Ovid (trans. Raeburn, David) *The Metamorphoses: a New Verse Translation*, London, Penguin Classics, 2004

Nennius (trans. Rowley, Richard) *Historia Britonum: The History of the Britons Attributed to Nennius,* Burnham-on-Sea, Llanerch Press, 2005

Pausanias (trans. Levi, Peter) *Pausanias Guide to Greece* Volume 2, London, Penguin Classics, 1971

Petronius (trans. Sullivan, John) *Petronius The Satyricon and the Fragments,* London, Penguin Classics, 1968

Plato (trans. Lee, H.D.P. and Lee, Desmond), *The Republic,* London, Penguin Classics, 2007

Pliny (trans. Rackham, H.) *Natural History*: Books 8–11, Cambridge, Loeb Classical Library, 1989

Rawlinson, George *The History of Herodotus,* New York, D. Appleton & Co, 1859

Remy, Nicolas (trans. Ashwin, E.A. and ed. Summers, Montague) *Demonolatry,* London, John Rodker, 1930

Rong, Jiang, *Wolf Totem,* London, Hamish Hamilton, 2008

Rosenstock, H.A. and Vincent, K.R. "A case of lycanthropy," *The American Journal of Psychiatry,* 134, 1147–1149, 1977

Rowling, J.K. 1999, *Harry Potter and the Prisoner of Azkaban,* London, Bloomsbury, 1999

Rowling, J.K. *Harry Potter and the Order of the Phoenix,* London, Bloomsbury, 2003

Rowling, J.K. *Harry Potter and the Half-Blood Prince,* London, Bloomsbury, 2005

Rowling, J.K. *Harry Potter and the Deathly Hallows,* London, Bloomsbury, 2007

Shakespeare, William (eds. Wells, S. and Taylor, G. and Jowett, J. and Montgomery, W.) *William Shakespeare: The Complete Works,* Oxford, Oxford University Press, 2005

Singh, Joseph Amrito Lal and Zingg, Robert M. *Wolf-Children and Feral Man,* Hamden, Archon Books, 1966

Skeat, Walter W. (trans.) *The Romance of William of Palerne: Otherwise Known as the Romance of William and the Werwolf; Also a Fragment of the Romance, Alisaunder,* Whitefish, Kessinger Publishing, 2007

Slemen, Thomas *Haunted Liverpool 3,* Liverpool, The Bluecoat Press, 2008

Stevenson, Robert Louis *The Strange Case of Dr Jekyll and Mr Hyde,* London, Penguin Classics, 2007

Taylor, Joules *Dream Decoder,* London, Godsfield Press, 2006

Verne, Jules *P'tit Bonhomme,* Paris, Bibliothèque d'Éducation et de Récréation. J. Hetzel et Cie, 1893

Virgil (trans. Lee, Guy) *The Eclogues,* London, Penguin Classics, 2006

Wratislaw, A.H. *Sixty Folk-Tales from Exclusively Slavonic Sources,* Charleston, BiblioBazaar, 2007

Further Reading

NON-FICTION

Baring-Gould, Sabine *The Book of Were-Wolves,* London, Smith Elder & Co, 1865
Although only the first ten chapters are directly relevant to werewolves, this useful collection of old stories and ideas is freely available on the internet from sites such as www.sacred-texts.com.

Cohen, Daniel *Werewolves,* New York, Dutton Juvenile, 1996
Written for children, this book offers a thorough introduction to werewolves.

Frost, Brian J. *The Essential Guide to Werewolf Literature,* Madison, WI, University of Wisconsin Press, 2003
As it says in the title, a comprehensive guide to fiction and non-fiction in print. Does not include any 21st-century titles.

Godfrey, Linda S. *Hunting the American Werewolf: Beast Men in Wisconsin and Beyond,* WI, Trails Media Group, 2006
This builds on the success of Linda Godfrey's 2003 study *The Beast of Bray Road,* and investigates a wide range of modern werewolf sightings in America.

Otten, Charlotte F (ed.) *A Lycanthropy Reader: Werewolves in Western Culture,* Syracuse NY, Syracuse University Press, 1986
A multidisciplinary, academic look at werewolfism, ranging from werewolves in fiction to medieval and Renaissance history.

Summers, Montague *The Werewolf in Lore and Legend,* Mineola, Dover Publications, 2003
A reprint of this classic compendium originally published as *The Werewolf* in 1933. Concentrating on the European werewolf tradition, this book's information is a bit scattered and many quotes are not translated, but there is no doubting the author's belief in the bodily transformation of the werewolf.

FICTION

Clamp, Cathy and C.T. Adams, *Hunter's Moon,* London, Tor Books, 2004
Focusing on a Mafia hit man who is a werewolf, this novel combines both suspense and romance in a supernatural setting. The sequel *Moon's Web* (2005) continues his story. Later books in this series introduce a wide range of shape-shifters.

Hayter, Sparkle *Naked Brunch,* New York, Three Rivers Press, 2003
This comedy revolves around a nice girl—bright but lonely—in a big city. Pandemonium ensues when she discovers she's a werewolf.

Huff, Tanya *Blood Trail,* New York, DAW Books, 1992
The second in a series of six books about a vampire, this particular book's focus is all about werewolves.

King, Stephen *Cycle of the Werewolf,* Detroit MI, Land of Enchantment, 1983
This book by the bestselling novelist was made into the movie *Silver Bullet* (1985.) Stephen King also features werewolves in the latter part of his book *The Talisman* (1984) written with Peter Straub.

Klause, Annette Curtis *Blood and Chocolate,* New York, Delacorte Press, 1997
This romantic mystery, written primarily for young adults and teens, features a female-lead character growing up in a werewolf pack in modern America.

Meyer, Stephenie *New Moon,* London, Little, Brown, 2006
This is the sequel to the vampire-focused *Twilight* (2006), and is followed by *Eclipse* (2007) and *Breaking Dawn* (2008). This best-selling series concentrates on the emotional life of its characters. In particular, *New Moon* offers an insight into the tense interpersonal relationships in a werewolf pack.

Scotch, Cheri *The Werewolf's Kiss,* New York, Diamond Books, 1992
This is the first in a trilogy about a clan of werewolves in New Orleans that face the challenge of family curses and voodoo magic. Subsequent books are *The Werewolf's Touch* (1993) and *The Werewolf's Sin* (1994), which features the return of the original tyrannical werewolf Lycaon.

Vaughn, Carrie *Kitty and the Midnight Hour,* New York, Grand Central Publishing, 2005
The first in an engaging series of thoroughly modern werewolf stories centering on a young, female werewolf—Kitty—who is cautiously stepping out of the shadows and bringing the existence of beings with "paranatural biology" to public attention. Other books in the Kitty series are: *Kitty Goes to Washington,* 2006; *Kitty Takes a Holiday,* 2007; *Kitty and the Silver Bullet,* 2008; *Kitty and the Dead Man's Hand,* 2009; and *Kitty Raises Hell,* 2009.

Index

Page numbers in *italics* indicate illustrations and captions. Definite and indefinite articles (A, An, The) at the beginning of titles have been ignored. An asterisk (*) indicates the name of a character in a book, movie, myth, or story.

PICTURE CREDITS

AKG 8, 35; British Library 147; **Alamy** Arco images GmbH 169; Mary Evans Picture Library 15, 27, 37, 139, 161; Photo12 7, 65, 75, 81, 91, 98, 108, 113; The London Art Archive 142; The Print Collector 23; **Corbis UK Ltd** Leonard de Selva 163; Bettmann 41, 49, 79, 152; Blue Lantern Studio 11; Chris Hellier 132; DLILLC 171; Kevin R Morris 20; Sandro Vannini 33; Sanford/agliolo 28; The Gallery Collection 129; Underwood and Underwood 70, 73; **Dover Publications** 24; **Getty Images** Hulton Archive 92; Redferns 16; **Photo12** Archives du 7eme 2, 54, 164; Collection Cinema 67, 167; **Picture Desk** Universal 53, 84; **Rex Features** Everett Collection 50; Lions Gate/Everett 115; Unapix/Everett 63, 101; **Science Photo Library** Georgette Douwma 169; **TopFoto** 121; Charles Walker 93, 94; Fortean 135, 158; FotoWare FotoStation 46, 59, 60, 172; Roger-Vollet 116; The Granger Collection 127, 157; **Touchpaper TV** Adrian Rogers 24.

Illustrations of the 'lupinone' molecule, and the magic square, are by Kai Taylor.